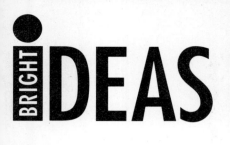 

Classroom Management

Written by Diane Montgomery and Anne Rawlings

Published by Scholastic Publications Ltd,
Marlborough House, Holly Walk,
Leamington Spa, Warwickshire CV32 4LS.
© 1986 Scholastic Publications Ltd
Reprinted 1987, 1988, 1989, 1990, 1991,
1992
Compiled by Diane Montgomery
and Anne Rawlings
Edited by Philip Steele
Sub-edited by Jackie Cunningham-Craig
Designed by David Cox
Illustrations by Sue Lines

Printed in Great Britain by
Loxley Brothers Ltd, Sheffield

ISBN 0-590-70602-0

Front and back cover: Martyn Chillmaid.

Contents

52 RESOURCE ORGANISATION

Introduction

Classroom Management includes the practical organisation of human and material resources in a home base called a 'classroom'. Good management can positively influence the way in which people interact and participate in school life. Although the ideas presented here are focused upon a classroom they can easily be used or adapted for any open plan setting as can the principles of managing the children. However the majority of primary teachers still work in classrooms and most of these have not been especially designed for present day needs. Primary classrooms are often located in buildings which have changed usage over the years. In many cases this presents problems in terms of space, access, furniture, teaching areas, light and sound as well as the interactions between people.

Classroom management skills are specific routines and actions which teachers can learn to use and so become more fully effective whatever views they hold on teaching style.

Teaching style is very much a personal matter. The way a teacher goes about things depends a great deal on the individual and his or her children. Some teachers are happy with a lot less structure than others. Whatever style is adopted, organisation of resources and equipment is of paramount importance. It is the key to taking advantage of spontaneous interest and seizing every 'teaching' opportunity. Accessibility of equipment is vital. It is no good spending valuable time and energy scurrying around hunting for bits and pieces during teaching time. Ideally, all that the children are likely to need should be ready to hand. This book sets out to help you organise yourself and the classroom more efficiently, from planning a flexible classroom layout to adapting a golf trolley for mobile storage.

Children should be encouraged to make a display of their work, so a wealth of suggestions have been included to put you on the right track. Hopefully these will act as a spring board for further ideas. Not only will they brighten and transform your classroom providing a happier environment but they will also encourage the children to take pride in their work.

An essential part of teaching is to record information for future reference – this will highlight areas needing more or less attention, problems with individual children and any hiccups in the curriculum. *Classroom Management* will show you how to do this without any fuss.

Useful hints and tips on classroom behaviour have also been included to ensure a more peaceful, stable atmosphere.

At the end of the book, you will find a selection of material: charts, timetables, standard forms and letters plus a diary of dates to remember. These may be photocopied for classroom use without infringement of copyright.

Any teacher, whether dipping in at random or studying at leisure, will find *Classroom Management* an invaluable tool in aiding the smooth running of their teaching life.

Diane Montgomery and Anne Rawlings

Classroom organisation

Storage and the organisation of equipment and resources

One of the most difficult aspects of the work which teachers have to cope with is storage and organisation of materials and equipment: there is seldom enough space or sufficient quantity of containers in most classrooms for the large numbers of individuals who have to use them. The overriding aim of teachers should be to encourage children to become as autonomous as possible. The more they can do for themselves, the fewer demands they will make on the teacher. This is especially important when it comes to getting out and putting away equipment in the correct places. Once a routine is established, with fixed positions and colour coding of shelves and materials, this becomes an easy pattern to maintain. It should not then be necessary for the teacher to have to spend time sorting out what the children have put away. Appointing monitors for fetching, carrying and tidying acts against the principle of making children responsible for their own work and keeping the classroom tidy. Therefore, monitor lists and charts are not recommended except on exceptional occasions. You will find a school stock list useful in organising your classroom (*see copy page 99*).

Parents as helpers in the classroom

Not all schools and headteachers are convinced that parents should be invited into school for any purpose except collecting and delivering children. Before bringing in parents as helpers it is a good idea to check on the school policy and practice so that you know the starting point. Bringing in parents and grandparents can be a great support to many projects you want to run, but remember that adults need to be shown exactly what to do and how to do it when working with small groups or individual children. Letters of invitation and thanks are essential, as are lists of materials the parents will need to use. Sequences of instructions and evaluation sheets are necessary if you are going to get the best out of parents, for the children's sakes. It is also preferable to arrange that the parents work with children other than their own. Detailed notes on parent help are on page 21.

Classroom layout

Age range
Three to twelve.

Group size
Large group or class.

What you need
Room measurements,
furniture measurements,
the intended
number of children.

What to do
Plan the layout of your room before your first day. First of all, take measurements. Design a rough plan on paper and then arrange your classroom accordingly. Change your design at, say, termly intervals. If you decide to have a teaching base, you must make sure that you have a clear view of the whole room. This should preferably be near the door, so that any strangers who wander in unannounced may be challenged. Although your base may be in one place, your teaching position may vary, depending on what you are teaching. This can be a helpful way of contacting more children than if you always teach from one position.

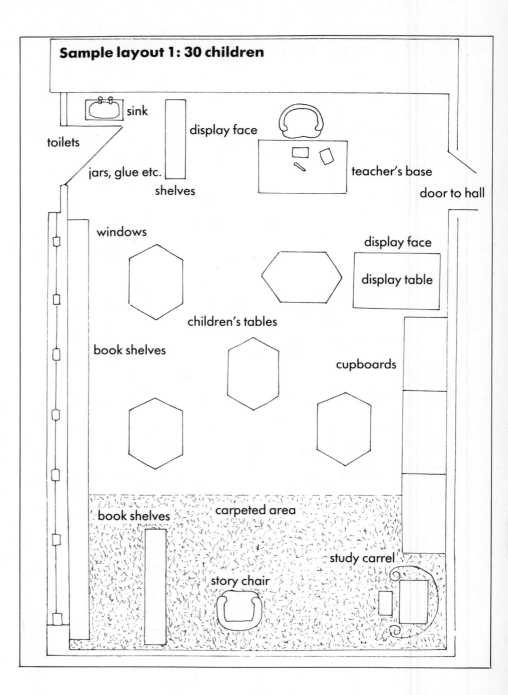

Sample layout 1: 30 children

sink
display face
toilets
jars, glue etc.
teacher's base
shelves
door to hall
windows
display face
display table
children's tables
book shelves
cupboards
book shelves
carpeted area
study carrel
story chair

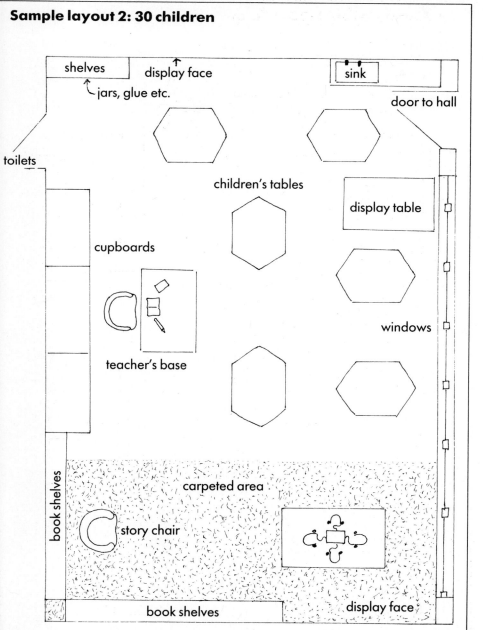

Sample layout 2: 30 children

shelves

display face

jars, glue etc.

sink

door to hall

toilets

children's tables

display table

cupboards

teacher's base

windows

book shelves

carpeted area

story chair

book shelves

display face

Note the 'action zones' indicated below. Children in the action zones receive more teacher attention and support, and so concentrate more and work harder. In this way, changing the teaching position increases the amount of active learning and support in your classroom. Do not change it continually, but plan your positioning by periods of time or by work requirements.

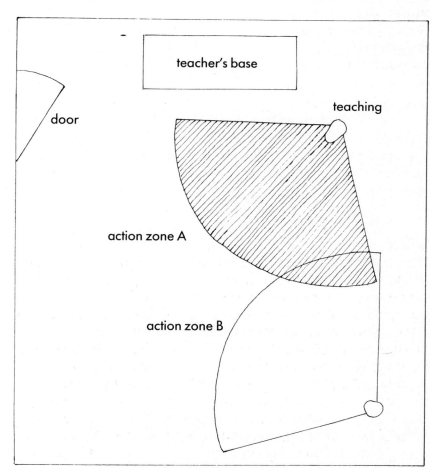

teacher's base

door

teaching

action zone A

action zone B

Planning for limited space

Age range
Three to twelve.

Group size
Classroom group.

What you need
Catalogue of school furniture,
extending tape measure,
squared paper.

What you do
Measure the area of your classroom and the large
cupboards and immovable objects in it, so that you can
draw it on to squared paper. This will enable you to plan
the types of table the room can house, and estimate the
number of children the room will comfortably hold.

GRID PLAN

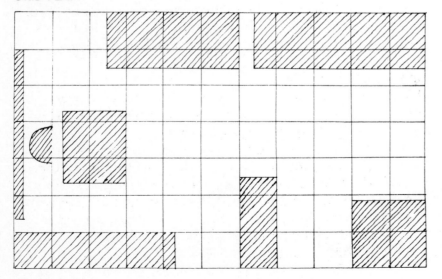

Large classes which have to be squeezed into small
rooms benefit from this pre-planning. Round tables (A)
use more space than rectangular or rhomboid tables and
prevent access around the classroom. With rhomboid
tables (B), children can easily have an identified place at
their table: gangways are left free for movement. The
rhomboid shapes enable them to be used flexibly,
singly or in pairs or clusters for different effects.

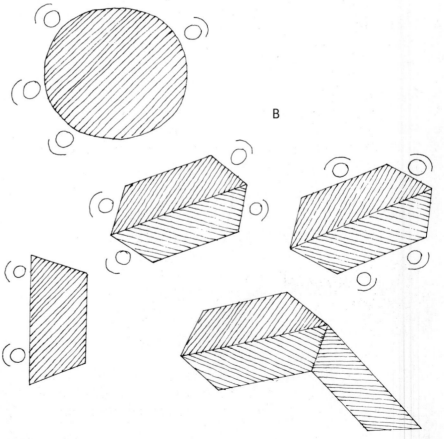

Table groupings

Age range
Three to twelve.

Group size
Class groups.

What you need
Movable tables and chairs.

What to do
Try different classroom groupings to suit the work in hand.

Vertical grouping
When there are several age groups in the class it is sometimes possible that work in maths and reading can be arranged so that younger able children can work with older children, and share ideas and experiences.

Mixed ability grouping
On other occasions organise groups of mixed ability, so that able children become used to helping less able ones and sharing with them. The brighter ones will stimulate and encourage the others. They can read along together, or paint or make models with one another.

Setting
As an alternative try changing the group membership in different areas so that groupings vary for language, mathematics, science, art, computer work, craft design.

Avoid persistent 'streaming' according to ability in reading and mathematics, otherwise children in the bottom ability groups will begin to feel failures and act like failures. Also avoid labels like 'the top table' or the 'slow table'.

Friendship grouping
Encourage friendship groups and patterns to develop and be flexible enough to allow children to exchange places when their friends change.

Random grouping
Often children do not have a home base or place in their classroom, but sit where they choose and change at any time. Starting off the term in this way may be useful. When organising activities such as painting and project work random grouping may be an effective use of space.

Special table grouping
It is often practical to prepare the morning's work by identifying specific tables for specific activities: a table or two where the task is language work, for example, which has all the equipment for writing, such as pencils and pens, rulers, writing books or folders containing writing paper. The table should be covered with sugar paper of the appropriate *colour code* for language work, eg red.

Mathematics tables, craft tables and painting areas can be set up in the same way. They can then move round to complete their allotted tasks.

Rows versus groups

Age range
Eight to twelve.

Group size
Class groups.

What you need
Set of rectangular tables or pairs of small square individual tables.

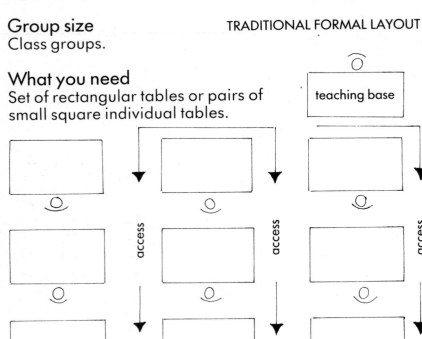

TRADITIONAL FORMAL LAYOUT

teaching base

access access access

What to do
Arrange your tables in rows down the classroom. When children are seated in rows, it is easier to control their movement and chatter, and to move down the gangways towards them. Children in rows are found to produce more work, but it cuts down on social and language interactions. Rows enable you to quieten difficult classes more easily: they are found in more formal classrooms.

Moving furniture

Age range
Three to twelve.

Group size
All groups.

What you need
Borrowed golf trolley elastic straps, help from caretaker.

What to do
Never move heavy furniture (particularly bookcases with books in them) on your own, or with the children. Empty the cupboards and shelves, and then ask the caretaker to move them for you on his special trolley. Avoid backstrain at all costs. For lighter furniture, a golf trolley can be used and save a lot of effort and strain. Either trolley can carry bagged or boxed-up books from one place to another.

Classroom screens

Age range
Three to twelve.

Group size
Large or small groups.

What you need
Garden trellis,
sticky tape,
or hammer and nails.

garden trellis

What to do
Areas can be made for special work or display by using garden trellis. It makes useful dividers, but does not obscure the teacher's or the children's view. Work can be easily attached to the trellis, which can also be used as an impromptu screen for puppet shows, etc. It is better to fix two pieces of trellis together with sticky tape, as this is easily removed when a change is required.

NB Be careful not to have too many dividers which might impede progress to doors and windows in case of fire. Remove trellis when conducting experiments with candles and matches.

Study carrels

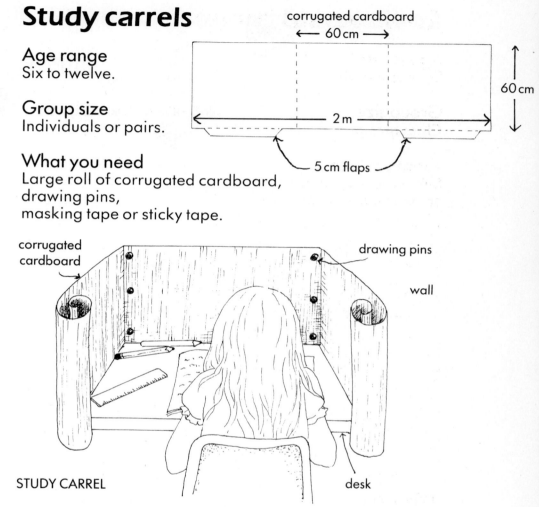

corrugated cardboard
← 60 cm →
60 cm
2 m
5 cm flaps

Age range
Six to twelve.

Group size
Individuals or pairs.

What you need
Large roll of corrugated cardboard,
drawing pins,
masking tape or sticky tape.

corrugated cardboard
drawing pins
wall
desk

STUDY CARREL

What to do
Cut a section 2 m long and 60 cm wide from the roll. Attach a central length of 60 cm to the wall or board with tape or drawing pins. Make 5 cm flaps on the side pieces as shown. Fold outwards and attach to the desk with tape along the desk surface. Do not make a flap on the back piece or it will curl.

Drying paintings

Age range
Three to twelve.

Group size
Large or small groups.

What you need
Circular foldaway line,
expanding clothes rack
or linen line,
pegs.

LINEN LINE (beware obstruction)

CIRCULAR FOLDAWAY LINE

EXPANDING CLOTHES RACK

What to do
Paintings are one of the most difficult large items to cope
with in the classroom, especially when they are wet.
Expanding clothes racks are ideal for storing many wet
paintings, and take up less room than having them strung
across the room on a clothes line. Hang very large
paintings over the arms, or peg lighter ones on to the
arms. If you peg them back to back, many more can be
dried at the same time.

   Stringing lines across the room can cause an
obstruction. If the line is too high it may go near the
electric lights and become a fire hazard. Take care.

Movable display walls

Age range
Three to twelve.

Group size
Large or small groups.

What you need
Large rolls of corrugated cardboard.

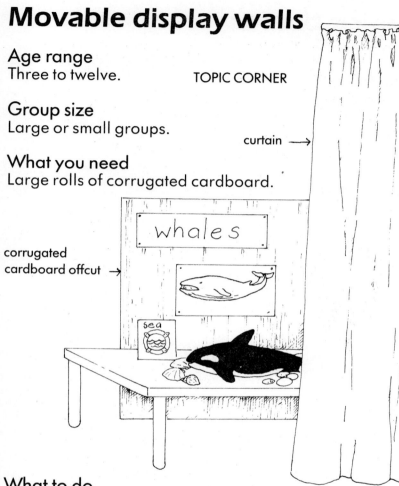

TOPIC CORNER

curtain →

whales

corrugated
cardboard offcut →

sea

What to do
The layout of the classroom can be varied, and sections remodelled, by using rolls of corrugated cardboard as movable walls and partitions. For instance you can create a new topic area by curtaining off a corner, and pinning an offcut section of the roll against the wall.

NB Do not stand a full, heavy roll in the middle of the room to be knocked over. Always use offcuts or light sections of cardboard.

A cover-up

Age range
Three to twelve.

Group size
Large or small groups.

What you need
Roll of corrugated cardboard (about 2m high).

corrugated cardboard

What to do
Poor decoration in the classroom can make for a depressing teaching environment. Lining the wall with corrugated cardboard can provide a more cheerful display area. The cardboard can be rapidly erected and easily dismantled.

Display for small people

Age range
Three to nine.

Group size
Large or small groups.

What you need
Large roll of
corrugated cardboard.

corrugated cardboard

What to do
Small people stand at a disadvantage in many
classrooms: space for display at eye-level is at a
premium. Paintings and all kinds of children's work can
easily be displayed on offcuts of corrugated cardboard.
This can easily rolled up and cleared away for another
activity. It will take staples, pins and glue.

Notice-boards

Age range
Seven to twelve.

Group size
All groups.

What you need
Coloured paper,
strips of wood.

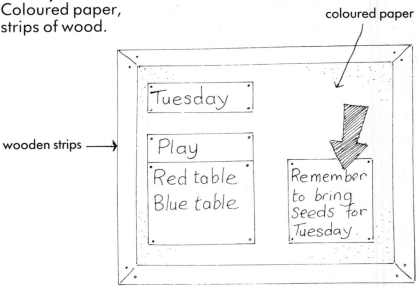

NOTICE-BOARD

coloured paper

wooden strips →

Tuesday

Play

Red table
Blue table

Remember
to bring
seeds for
Tuesday.

What to do
A special section of wall board or wall space can be set
aside for 'jobs of work', charts and timetables. These can
be posted daily for younger children and weekly for
older ones.
   Line a rectangular space (say 50 × 60 cm) with brightly
coloured paper and pin thin strips of wood round it to
make it look like a special notice-board. Specially
important notices can be indicated by a red arrow.

Arranging shelves

Age range
Three to twelve.

Group size
All groups.

What you need
Large sheets of coloured lining paper, shelving, or surfaces which can be used as shelves (eg short planks, supported by wood, bricks or breezeblocks).

coloured lining paper →

What to do
Decide which colour is going to be a base colour for each of the different curriculum areas. Line the shelves with the appropriate colour. This gives children who have difficulty in reading a visual aid to find equipment: eg mathematics equipment – blue; creative equipment – yellow; reading and writing materials – red.

If you have a limited amount of shelving this can be added to in various ways, quite safely, by using solid blocks of wood (offcuts from joineries), or bricks or breezeblocks from builders to support planks. Leave spaces for work trays underneath.

NB Be careful not to build such additional shelving up too high, or with protruding ends which might be jerked away from the base when books and trays are being collected.

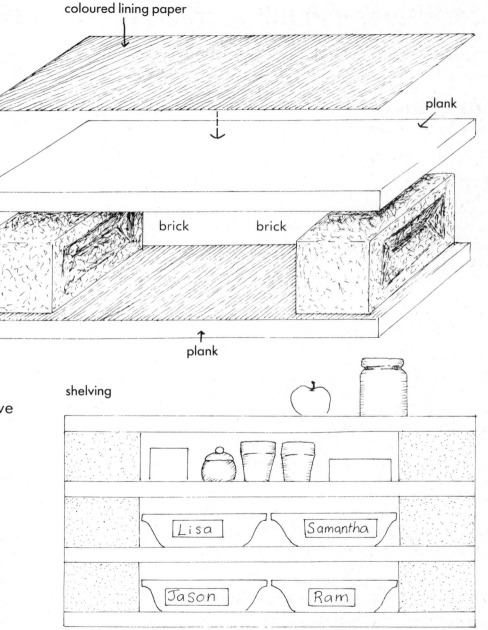

coloured lining paper

plank

brick   brick

plank

shelving

Lisa   Samantha

Jason   Ram

Cabinets of trays

Age range
Three to twelve.

Group size
Individuals.

What you need
Catalogue of school furniture,
sticky labels.

CABINET STORAGE

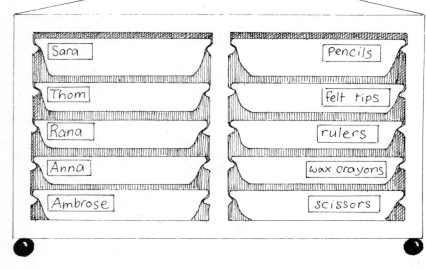

What to do
Label the trays with individual children's names, and allow them to keep their books and pencils in the trays. Alternatively, extra cupboards of these trays can be used for storing materials.

These cupboards of trays are useful when the tables need to be used very flexibly and the floor space is not at a premium.

Personal trays

Age range
Three to twelve.

Group size
Individuals.

What you need
Catalogue of school furniture.

PERSONAL DESK STORAGE

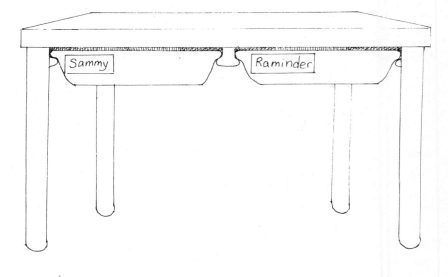

What to do
Do you have a shortage of floor space for the size of the class in the room? If you have the opportunity to choose or exchange furniture, you can bring in tables which have personal slide-under trays, in which the children can keep their personal effects and books. This means that the wall cupboard which formerly housed such trays can be removed and so give more floor space.

Paper storage

Age range
Three to twelve.

Group size
Large or small groups.

What you need
Kitchen paper,
sharp knife.

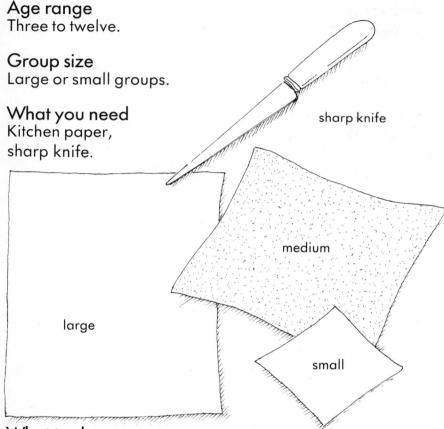

sharp knife

medium

large

small

What to do
Paper soon becomes dog-eared and shabby if not stored correctly. Paper such as kitchen or computer paper can easily be pre-cut into three different sizes (large, medium and small) with a sharp knife. This will encourage children to think about the size of the drawing or painting they want to do, and help them to build concepts about 'large', 'medium' and 'small'. This is particularly valuable for children in the younger age groups.

Tissue paper storage

Age range
Three to twelve.

Group size
Large or small groups.

What you need
Tissue paper,
sharp knife.

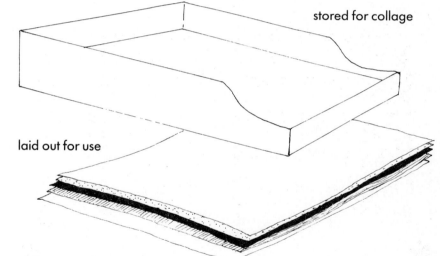

stored for collage

laid out for use

What to do
Tissue paper comes packed in quires or folded, which makes it difficult to see the variety of colours. If a little time is spent separating the sheets and laying out a small portion of them individually, one can easily see the colours, and only one sheet at a time will be used. Some tissue paper can be cut into different sizes and stored for collage work. Always cut tissue paper with a knife: it is much quicker than using scissors.

Storing lunch boxes

Age range
Three to twelve.

Group size
Large or small groups.

What you need
Portable library trolley,
name labels.

trolley

What to do
Great distress and confusion can arise over finding the
correct lunch box. The trolley is one of the most successful
methods of storing these lunch boxes. It is important that
the children's lunch boxes are stored off the ground and
preferably on a shelf, in view of an adult. The trolley can
always be in view. One side can be used for books and
the other side for lunch boxes: this makes it easy for the
children to have access to apples etc at lunch breaks,
and eliminates delving into deep containers searching
for one's own box, and problems such as knocking off
lids of others and spilling the contents.

Secondary schools with Craft/Design/Technology
departments often take projects such as this one as an
exercise in practical problem-solving.

Colour-coded book corner

Age range
1 Three to eight;
2 Eight to twelve.

Group size
Class groups.

What you need
Sheets of paper
(at least four different colours),
sticky tape or
coloured insulating tape
(red, yellow, blue, green,
white and black are
generally available),
scissors.

colour code ⟶

What to do
1 Grade the books into the categories for which they are
  suitable: very young children (red); those beginning to
  read (blue); early stages of reading (yellow), and
  general readers for six to seven year olds (green).
  Stick the coloured paper on to the spines of the books,
  using the sticky tape to hold the paper down, or use
  coloured insulating tape.
2 For the eight to twelve year olds it is possible to use a
  readability formula such as SMOG (Simple Measure
  of Gobbledygook) or Fry's readability formula to find
  the reading age of the books' contents and the colour
  code in age levels. Children can then be encouraged
  to select the appropriate levels of book according to
  colour code suitable for their reading age.

Guidelines for parent help

Age range
Three to eight.
Helpers are used less often
for the seven to twelve age range
but the same rules apply.

Group size
Groups of three or four children.

What you need
Letter to parents (*see page 113*),
lesson plan, evaluation sheet
(*see page 110*).

What to do
Thorough organisation, detailed planning and a welcoming atmosphere are vital in encouraging parents to take part in classroom activities. Always make sure a letter is sent home to the parents involved, stating date, time and place etc. Meetings to discuss activities have to be arranged well in advance and it is essential that you have sufficient people available before embarking on a topic, outing or activity which requires many hands.

1 It is always a good idea to send thank you letters to parents who have been involved in school activities.
2 Working notes should be drawn up, circulated, discussed and amended, so that everyone is familiar and at ease with the format.
3 Listing the equipment to be used by the side of each activity provides a useful check list (*see page 110*).
4 Provide the parents with an agenda to follow, so that each step can be followed through.
5 Provide the parents with a list of words related to the topic (eg in baking bread, 'kneading', 'rolling', etc) demonstrating that their use is especially important for young children and others with special needs. It may be a good idea for the teacher to decide how a special need might be met before starting on a topic (*see page 110*).

A large part of success or failure will depend upon presentation. The most interesting activities can fall flat unless given an exciting delivery. Show some finished products to give an idea of what can be achieved and what might go wrong.
Encourage parents to:

- inject work with a sense of mystery, and adopt a 'what is going to happen next?' attitude;
- learn not to give the children all the answers, but allow them to follow through with ideas.

Parents and reading

Age range
Five to eleven.

Group size
Individual help.

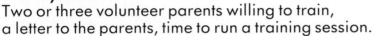

What you need
Two or three volunteer parents willing to train,
a letter to the parents, time to run a training session.

What to do
For paired reading in school, the parent (not necessarily
related to the child) sits with an individual child and they
read aloud together, quietly. This helps particularly in the
early stages of reading. The adult synchronises his or her
reading with the child's. If the child stumbles, the adult
reads quietly on and the child should join in. If he or she
does not, the adult should stop, and start together again.

When the child feels able to take over and read alone,
she or he makes a prearranged non-verbal signal, eg a
raised hand.

On seeing the signal, the adult stops reading and the
child continues alone. If the child's reading falters, the
adult joins in again. Nothing is said. When the piece is
finished the adult should praise the child. The child
should feel in control and stop reading, or stop the adult,
whenever she or he wishes.

Encourage parents to conclude their activities with an
evaluation, using a special sheet (*see page 110*).
Give a copy of your general lesson plan to the parent so
that you will both follow a similar procedure.

All parents should be encouraged to do paired
reading with their children at home. They should sit
together in a comfortable chair and read for a few
minutes each day using the same strategies as used in
school with parent helpers. Run a training programme
and make a booklet for parents to take away explaining
what to do (*see page 115*).

Story chair

Age range
Three to eight.

Group size
Class,
small groups
or pairs.

What you need
Wide armchair,
cloth offcut,
impact stapler.

Stories should be read at a regular time each day, perhaps at the end of the morning or afternoon, or even both where it is unusual for children to be read to at home. Children enjoy regularity and routine. Choose stories with plenty of opportunity for participation, especially when reading to groups of younger children.

What to do
The story chair should be wide enough for two children, or a child and teacher/parent, to sit together. It should have arms, and be comfortably padded. No one should be allowed to sit in the story chair unless they are going to tell or read a story. If the chair is old and threadbare, it can be easily covered with some colourful material: an offcut of curtain material will do. Cut it to a size just larger than the chair and attach the material with a staple-gun.

23

Making job charts

Age range
Three to eight.

Group size
To suit the class.

What you need
Large sheet of stiff card,
strips of thinner card
(possibly in a different colour),
scissors,
masking tape.

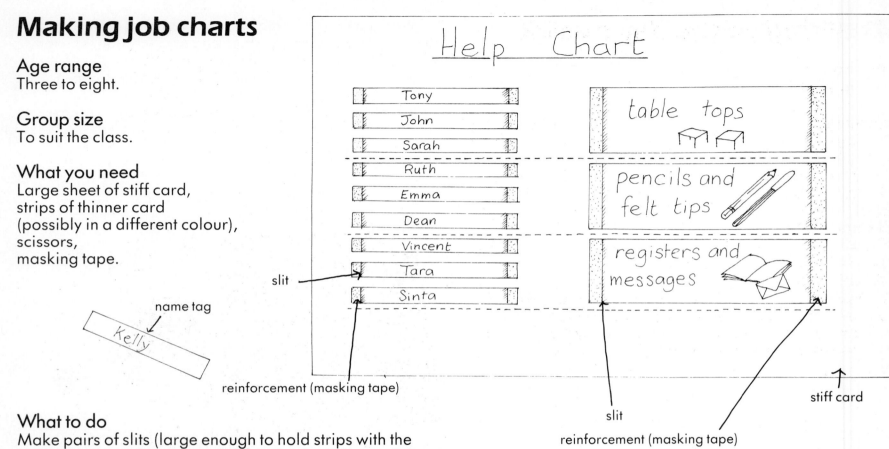

What to do
Make pairs of slits (large enough to hold strips with the children's names) down the left hand side of the card. On the right hand side, make larger pairs of slits to hold the cards which show the type of help needed and where needed. To be able to use this chart card regularly, bind the slits and the edge of the whole chart card with masking tape. Try to make the job charts as adaptable to general needs as you possibly can.

Thread the name slips and job slips through the pairs of slits as shown. Give picture clues to each job. Job charts are often very useful for when there is a lot of clearing up in, for example, painting and collage lessons.

24

Chalking up the day's work

Age range
Five to eight.

Group size
Class group.

What you need
A child's easel,
pegs,
blackboard
chalks.

What you do
Write up a list of tasks to be undertaken during the day
on the easel. The children can then choose the order they
will do the tasks in. At other times of the day the easel can
be used for practising writing and letter shapes.

easel

blackboard →

June 3rd
Monday
1. Write Diary
2. Number bonds
3. Paired reading
4. Finish paintings

Work folders

Age range
Five to twelve.

Group size
Class group.

What you need
Cards,
folders or
wallets.

What to do
Another way to present the day's work is for each child to collect their own work programme, which is written out on cards put into their folders. They then select the order in which they carry out the work.

PROGRAMME CARDS

WORK FOLDER

TUESDAY

Julie's programme

1) Find the 3 smallest children in the class

2) Make a barchart of their heights

3) Write a story about a tiny person visiting the classroom — an elf

4) Draw and paint your elf

Roller chart

Age range
Five to twelve.

Group size
Class group.

What you need
Dowelling or
broom-handle section,
roll of wallpaper
or lining paper,
hooks or string,
marker pen.

Flip chart

Age range
Five to twelve.

Group size
Class group.

What you need
Tray,
drawing board,
computer print-out
paper,
drawing pins.

string

roll

dowelling

marker

June 3rd Monday
1) Write Diary
2) 3 Measuring cards
— smaller
3) Small Clay man
4) Story of clay man journey

fold over or tear off

drawing pins

June 3rd Monday
1) Write diary
2) 3 measuring cards
— smaller
3) Small clay man
4) Story of clay man
journey

drawing board

paper

What to do
A roller chart is a good way to display information or
instructions such as work programmes. Use hooks or
string to suspend a length of dowelling or similar rod: this
holds a roll of lining paper or wallpaper. Brightly
coloured or patterned wallpaper does not provide a
suitable background for writing, but can be rewound with
the backing to the front. Use a marker pen for writing,
and tear off as necessary.

What to do
The daily work programme, or indeed any other
information, may be clearly displayed by means of a flip
chart. Pin sheets of paper to the top edge of a drawing
board. As you use the paper, tear it off sheet by sheet or
fold it back.

Presentation and display

Children's presentation

Children should grow up accustomed to taking care in the way they present their work, and to regard its appearance as an important aspect of the whole production. Encourage them to make their display convey in visual terms what the work is about.

Setting up a display

Utilising optimum space when setting up displays is of paramount importance, especially in smaller classrooms or hall areas. There are several key features to keep in mind when displaying children's work, whether it is for an open meeting, or in the school for the children only. Well-presented, eye-catching displays can set the standard for the school and the children, and usually they are the first thing visitors notice. It is therefore important to make sure that any work done by the children is displayed to its best advantage. The following points should be kept in mind when setting up a display:

1 Who is the display for?
2 Try to keep children's work at eye level.
3 Displays should encourage reading, listening, and touching as well as looking: notices and items to touch should be at the child's level. Make use of old fish tanks if you want children to look but not touch.
4 Titles and lettering should be large and attractive.
5 Always double mount pictures.
6 Link work through colours, or coordinate colours for a striking effect.
7 Make use of different-textured materials and crêpe paper to soften harsh lines.
8 Themes of work can be reflected in presentation.
9 Positioning is important: 3D displays have more impact if they are in a prominent position, in the centre of a room or large hall, for example.

Display tips

Letters which are cut from magazines, newspapers, and advertisements look very professional and add to a piece of work which could do with some help. All children should have some work on display and it is up to the teacher to see that the most is made of work done by the less able child.

Avoid visible sticky tape, ragged edges and drawing pins. Double sticky tape over to form a loop and apply to the back of work, or use double-sided sticky tape. Ordinary pins are less obtrusive (a 'pin pusher', easily obtained from any DIY shop, is a great help). Pins are more easily removed when the display comes down.

Don't leave any display up too long. Save the materials carefully so that you will have a selection to choose from for Open Day. Remember that the real purpose of good display is to show children that their work is important, that it matters, that other people want to see it and that therefore it is worth doing their very best.

display off-centre

double mounting

Mounting work

There is a greater satisfaction in visual terms when you leave a larger margin at the bottom of a picture than at the sides and top.

Unusual positioning can catch the eye or draw interest and attention to the display.

Large display areas

Age range
Three to twelve.

Group size
All groups.

What you need
Paint tins,
paint trays
(eg baking trays,
mixing bowls,
or cut down plastic 5-litre
containers)
cylindrical containers
(eg detergent containers,
dried milk powder containers),
sponge offcuts
about ½ cm to 1 cm thick),
elastic bands,
or paint rollers,
dowelling (½ cm in diameter),
or car sponge.

What to do
Large display areas will benefit immeasurably from a quick coat of paint. Cover the area with the mixed paint. Use a paint roller and tray, or make your own roller from the equipment shown below. Push the dowelling through the empty milk powder tin or other closed cylinder. Wrap a layer of foam sponge over this 'roller', and secure with elastic bands. Make sure that the cylinder will drip into the tray or plastic container, and allow excess liquid to be rolled off against the side or on a drip tray placed alongside.

Alternatively, use a large car sponge and thinly mixed powder paint. Dip and squeeze out the sponge in the paint, and cover large areas with steady sweeps of the sponge.

HOME-MADE ROLLER

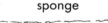
sponge

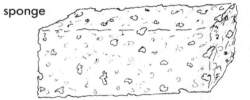

elastic band   sponge   cylinder

dowelling

drip tray

paint tray

30

Templates for display

Age range
Three to twelve.

Group size
All groups.

What you need
Lining paper,
card for templates,
scissors,
leaves,
paper doily or plate.

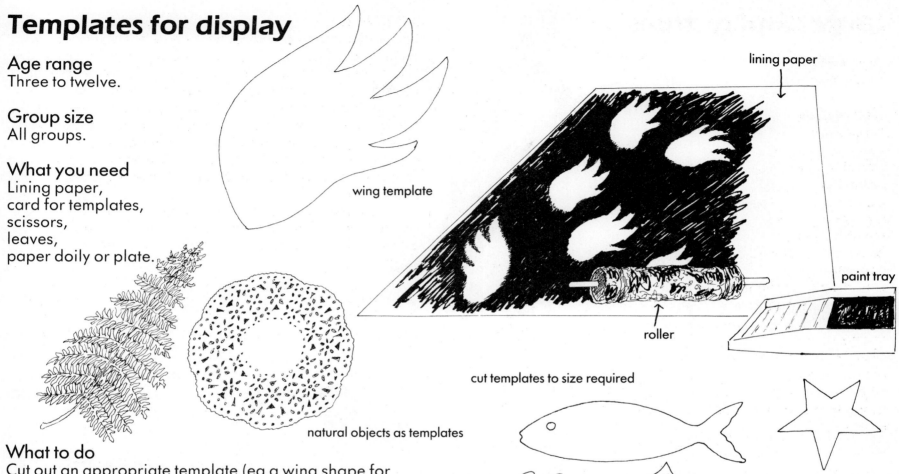

wing template

lining paper

paint tray

roller

natural objects as templates

cut templates to size required

What to do
Cut out an appropriate template (eg a wing shape for work on flight) and then place it at random positions on the large sheet of paper and roll over the shape each time with the roller.

After putting up the lining paper, use the appropriate template and spray the background. Make sure you do this with open windows to clear the air.

Many ordinary objects also make useful templates, eg a large fern leaf, a rubber-plant leaf, a paper doily, or paper plates.

Words and pictures

Age range
Three to twelve.

Group size
All groups
and individuals.

What you need
Card for templates,
scissors,
lining paper.

SHAPES

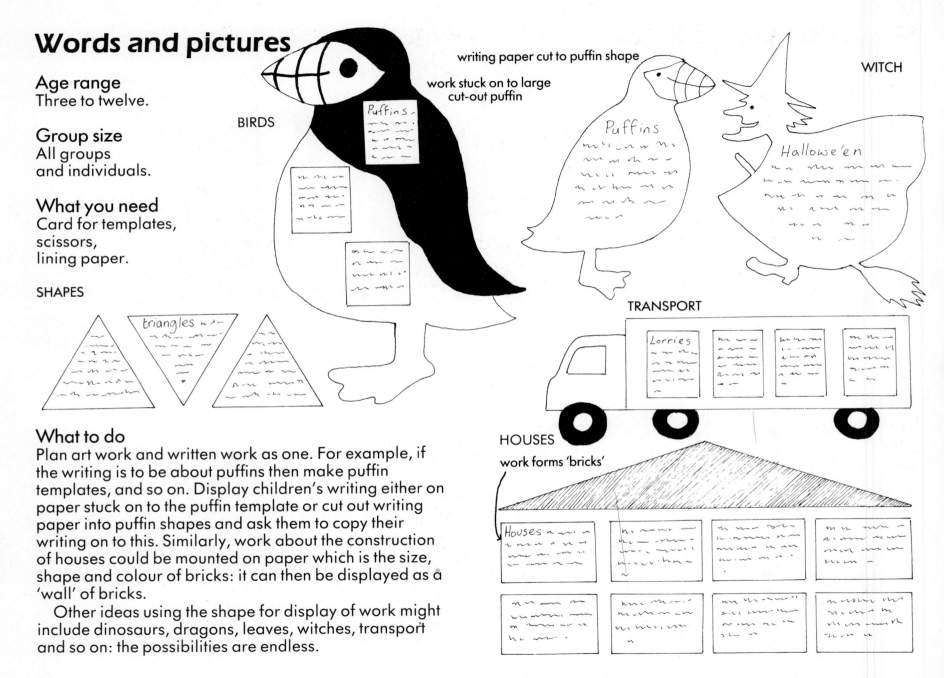

writing paper cut to puffin shape

work stuck on to large
cut-out puffin

BIRDS

WITCH

Puffins

Halloween

TRANSPORT

Lorries

HOUSES
work forms 'bricks'

Houses

triangles

What to do
Plan art work and written work as one. For example, if
the writing is to be about puffins then make puffin
templates, and so on. Display children's writing either on
paper stuck on to the puffin template or cut out writing
paper into puffin shapes and ask them to copy their
writing on to this. Similarly, work about the construction
of houses could be mounted on paper which is the size,
shape and colour of bricks: it can then be displayed as a
'wall' of bricks.

  Other ideas using the shape for display of work might
include dinosaurs, dragons, leaves, witches, transport
and so on: the possibilities are endless.

Silhouettes and friezes

Age range
Three to twelve.

Group size
All groups
and individuals.

What you need
Black spray paint or
black paint and roller,
thin card,
paper in various colours.

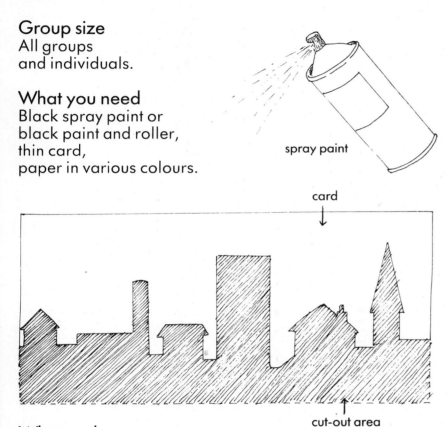

spray paint

card

cut-out area

What to do
Cut out the silhouette you wish to make from the card. By
placing the card over a sheet of dark blue paper, and
spraying or rolling on black paint, a city's night skyline
can be produced as a display sheet, or as a frieze round
part of the room. Orange backing paper produces a
contrasting 'sunset' effect.

Firework night displays

Age range
Three to twelve.

Group size
All groups
and individuals.

What you need
Card, pencil,
scissors,
black paper,
orange, red or
white
paint.

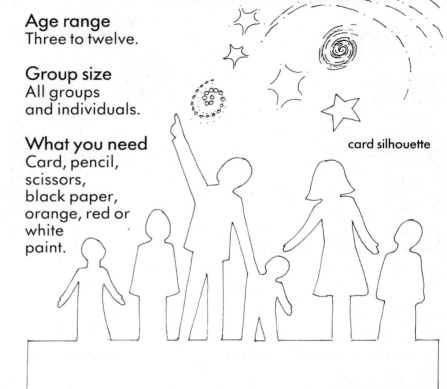

card silhouette

What to do
Draw a simple set of people shapes on card and cut them
out as above. Place the silhouettes over the black paper,
and spray lightly over them with the orange paint. Lightly
spray round the outside of the orange glow with red. The
children can then decorate the prepared paper with
fireworks or writing, or try the silhouette technique
themselves. For a winter alternative use black paper and
white paint to make a bus queue waiting in the snow. Add
a bus stop sign, and spray or roll over the silhouette with
white paint on black paper.

Lettering

Age range
Three to twelve.

Group size
All groups.

What you need
Coloured adhesive discs
or paper discs
and glue,
pre-cut paper triangles
(1 or 3 cm high),
coloured felt tips
(round- and square-tipped),
pencil,
rules.

What to do
Quick and effective lettering is crucial to your display.
Make a point of looking at typefaces used elsewhere and
take your inspiration from them. Picture lettering
appropriate to the subject is good with young children,
also geometric shapes (*see pages 126–127*).

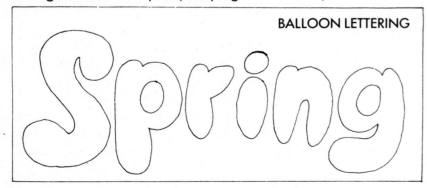

BALLOON LETTERING

PICTURE LETTERING

We like to look for
Frogspawn
in the pond

icy

Easter
Eggs

elephant   WORD SHAPES

bed

eagle

fish

Colouring over a large letter shape with a thick felt tip makes it stand out boldly in contrast to the others.

Large and small letter stencils (both upper and lower case) can be bought fairly cheaply at stationers', design shops and some do-it-yourself stores.

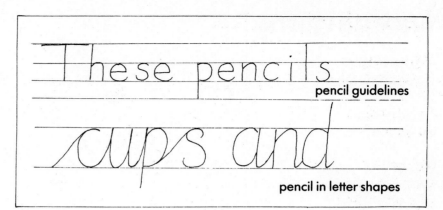

pencil guidelines

pencil in letter shapes

Felt tips are indispensable for displaying work. It is a good idea to pencil in the letters first to ensure that they will fit on to the sheet, and that size and spacing are even. Make sure pencil lines are horizontal. Use the pens confidently. For an italic style, use a square-tipped pen. Hold it at the same angle, without allowing it to move, as you trace over the pencil outline. This will give a consistent thick- and thin-stroke effect.

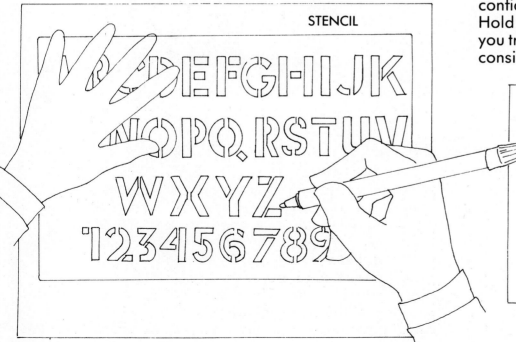

STENCIL

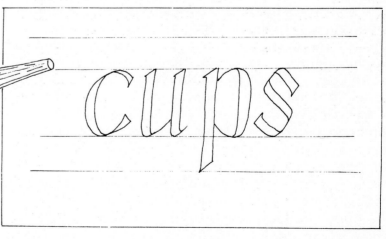

Wax patterns

Age range
Three to twelve.

Group size
Individuals.

What you need
Coarse sandpaper,
sheets of card,
thick wax crayons,
white drawing paper,
hot iron,
and black ink
(with a little water added).

What to do
Begin the pattern (1) by drawing on to a sheet of
coarse sandpaper, using a sheet of card as protection for
the fingers while working. Draw the design in bright
colours using thick wax crayons. Work the wax into the
rough surface of the sandpaper. When the design is
finished the rough surface should be covered with a sheet
of white drawing paper (2). Now iron with a lifting
motion using a hot iron (3). Rubbing the surface of the
paper can smear the design.

When the whole pattern has been ironed and the paper
removed, two pictures have been produced. The pattern
on the sandpaper (4) now has something of the
appearance of an oil painting due to the wax melting and
becoming polished. The one on the plain sheet of
paper (5) is covered with an attractive design. To
complete this new pattern, brush over with black ink to
which a little water has been added. The wax resists the
ink, resulting in a most attractive finished pattern.

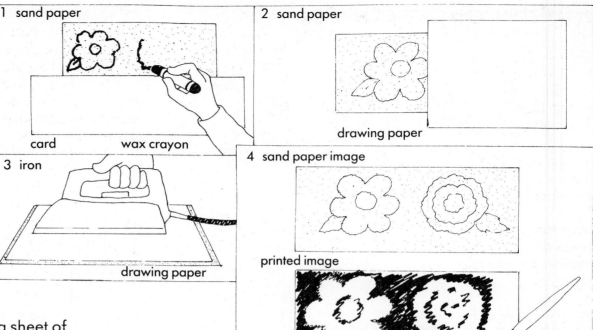

The children can create most outstanding displays of
wax-resist paintings. The secret of good wax-resist
paintings is to press really hard with the crayons when
doing the drawing. This may mean going over the
drawing several times, as small hands soon become tired
when pressing hard for any length of time. Make sure you
are not doing a writing activity soon after this art work.

Using black sugar paper as a background helps to
give a more 3D effect. This is more successful with the
younger children, as it enables them to create an effect
without covering every piece of paper with black ink.

Brighter display tables

Age range
Three to twelve.

Group size
All groups.

What you need
Thin card
or thick paper,
glue,
sticky tape,
scissors,
colouring materials,
tissue paper,
pins,
empty yoghurt pots,
stick or cane,
Plasticine,
pebbles or
damp sand,
gummed spots,
glitter,
crêpe paper,
cardboard rolls,
paper doilies.

What to do
Brighten up your display tables with material or crêpe paper. Paper doilies can be used to help highlight objects on display. Handicraft flowers and trees can add colour.

For a flower, first cover a yoghurt pot with paper, so that it can easily be painted. Cut 15 tissue circles, 12 cm across, in contrasting colours. Stick six or seven spots around the edge, or decorate with glitter. Fix a blob of Plasticine to the top of a stick. Fold a tissue circle into quarters, but do not make hard creases. Stick a pin through the middle of the circle and into the Plasticine. Continue in the same way with the other circles until you have finished. Fix the tree into the yoghurt pot, which should be filled with Plasticine, pebbles or damp sand.

For a fir tree use a cardboard roll or a cylinder of stiff paper to make a trunk. Cut circles of paper as shown to form the foliage. Colour and decorate; fringe the paper.

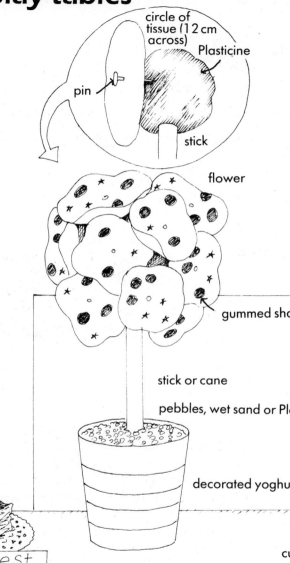

circle of tissue (12 cm across)

Plasticine

pin

stick

flower

gummed shapes

stick or cane

pebbles, wet sand or Plasticine

decorated yoghurt pot

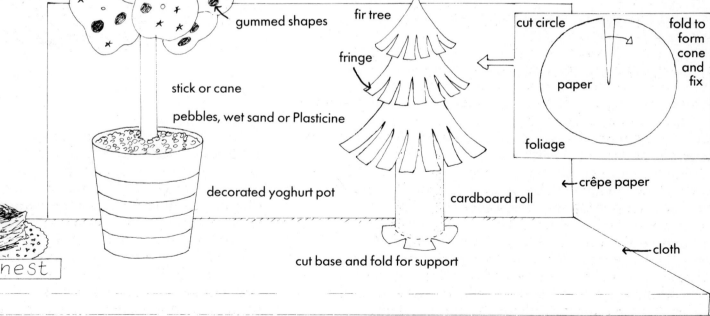

fir tree

fringe

cut circle

fold to form cone and fix

paper

foliage

crêpe paper

cardboard roll

cut base and fold for support

cloth

paper doily

nest

Surprises

Age range
Five to eleven.

Group size
Individuals.

What you need
Thirty 15 cm-square cards.

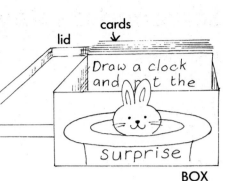

What to do
Number the cards 1–30 and stand them on end in a shoe box. On each card put a different task. Make the instructions brief: eg 'Draw a clock and put the time on it'; 'Get a book about animals, and draw three of them'; 'Tidy the pencils'; 'Choose your favourite story in the classroom and read it quietly in the book corner'.

Tell the children they must always take from the front and put the card back at the rear of the box.

Have a surprise box corner and put in it a variety of objects such as a box of shapes, magnets, old clocks etc.

SURPRISE CORNER DISPLAY

Decorated boards

Age range
Three to twelve.

Group size
All groups.

What you need
Crêpe paper,
children's pictures,
scissors.

What to do
To create different effects, crêpe paper can be trimmed in many ways. Cut a curved edge to give a wavy effect, or cut a jagged edge to give an icy effect. Cut strips of crêpe paper and attach to the board diagonally before putting up paintings.

Group pictures of various sizes and shapes together to save space. Some pictures can be overlapped at corners. Always label paintings etc with the child's name.

For interesting borders, roll the crêpe paper into tubes and cut according to your design, eg autumn leaves. Nothing looks worse than a 'raggy' edge. To make the edges of the board look attractive cut crêpe paper with the desired edging.

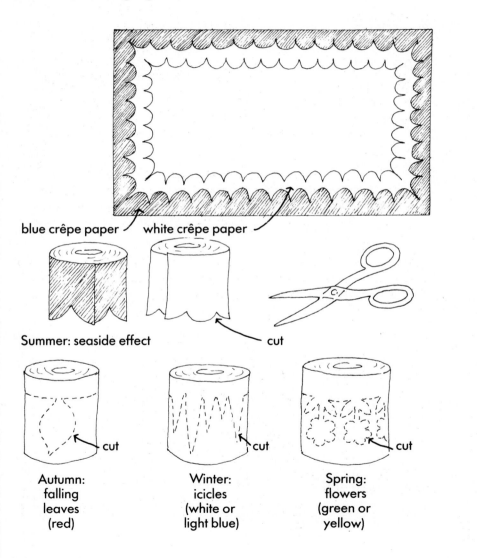

blue crêpe paper   white crêpe paper

Summer: seaside effect   cut

Autumn:
falling
leaves
(red)

Winter:
icicles
(white or
light blue)   cut

Spring:
flowers
(green or
yellow)   cut

Screened displays

Age range
Three to twelve.

Group size
All groups.

What you need
Display stands
or curtain screens
or plywood boards
and wood for feet
(10 × 2.5 × 40 cm),
saw,
wood glue,
brackets,
screws,
screwdriver.

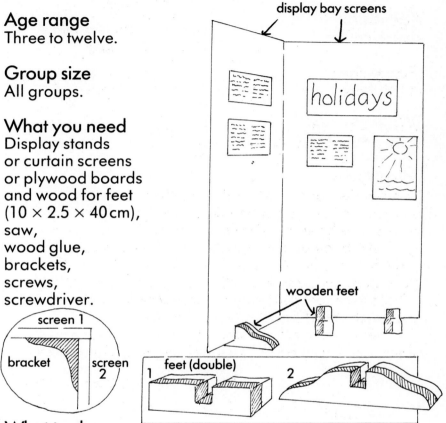

display bay screens

holidays

wooden feet

screen 1

bracket   screen 2

feet (double)   1   2

What to do
To make a special display bay, look for display stands, curtained screens (on wheels) or large boards left behind by builders. Use two boards or screens to make a special corner. It may be possible simply to place proper screens together or to bracket them securely. Home-made screens made from plywood boards will need fixing together and supporting at the base. For this purpose, cut feet as shown from lengths of wood. Stick two together for strength. They can be used time and time again.

Cupboard display

Age range
Three to twelve.

Group size
All groups.

What you need
Sugar paper
(for lining),
drawing pins.

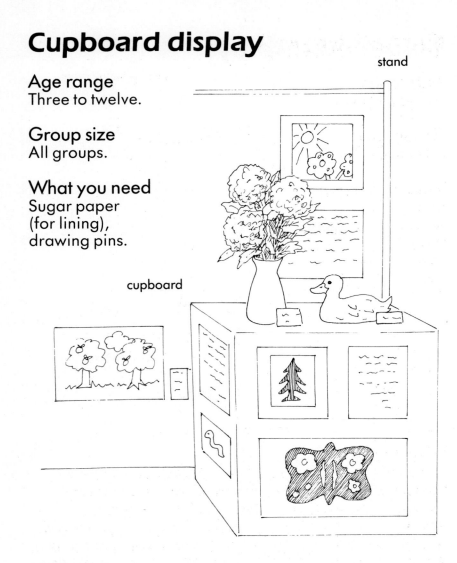

What to do
Move cupboards to a position at right angles to the wall or screens, in order to make a small display bay. You can then line the back of the cupboard with sugar paper and use it as a display space.

Trellis display

Age range
Three to twelve.

Group size
All groups.

What you need
Garden trellis,
low cupboard
or bookshelf,
a bamboo cane,
dowel rod
or broom handle,
string.

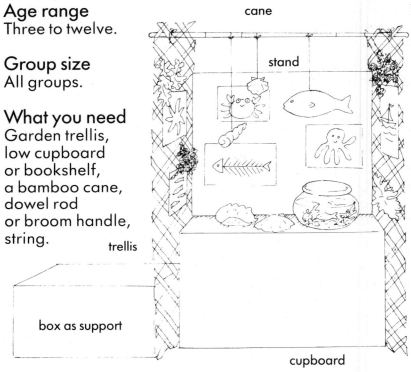

What to do
Stand two pieces of trellis on end each side of a low cupboard or bookshelf. Sandwich the lower sections on each side of the trellis with a box, table or bookcase to hold them firmly erect. In some circumstances it may be possible to use screws to attach the trellis on each side to the cupboard, and so avoid the need for support.

A bamboo cane tied between the two upper parts of the trellis gives added strength and support. Pictures and all kinds of children's work can be hung on to trellis and displayed in this special bay. One child's work across the curriculum might be shown in this way.

Table and board display

Age range
Three to twelve.

Group size
All groups.

What you need
Hardboard
or chipboard
or thick cardboard
or corrugated
cardboard,
lining paper.

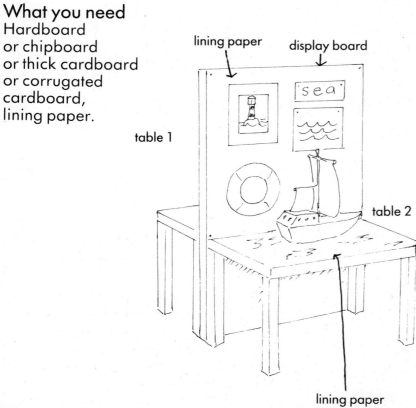

table 1

lining paper

display board

sea

table 2

lining paper

What to do
For a simple and effective display, sandwich the board between two tables. Cover each side with the lining paper and put up the display.

Curtaining off

Age range
Three to twelve.

Group size
All groups.

What you need
Cup hook,
short rod,
string,
fabric for hanging.

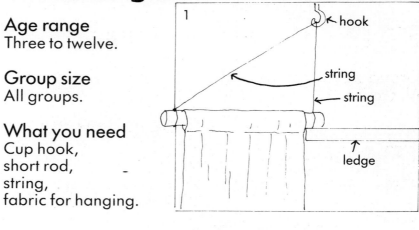

hook

string

string

ledge

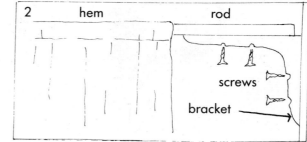

hem

rod

screws

bracket

What to do
A curtain can create an excellent display bay. Fix a cup hook into the wall, or the woodwork of the picture rail. Tie a string to each end of the rod after threading it through the hem on the curtain (1). There are alternative ways of fixing a hanging fabric. For example, you might attach the fabric to the side of a cupboard with drawing pins. You might also use a metal shelf support and screws. Attach the curtain rod to one arm of the bracket and fix the other arm to a secure piece of wood which runs horizontally along the wall, such as a wall board frame. Display the work on the curtain.

Block display

Age range
Three to twelve.

Group size
All groups.

What you need
Assorted large boxes, large pieces of fabric, drawing pins, sticky tape.

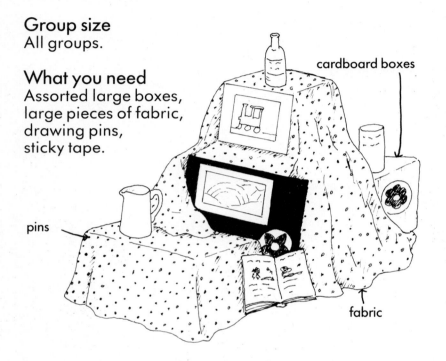

cardboard boxes

pins

fabric

What to do
Large boxes can provide a useful display base. Check them to see that they are strong enough to support small weights without collapsing. Seal down each box with sticky tape to lend strength. Put the sealed ends vertically and build up the boxes, one on top of the other, to the desired shape. Attach the boxes together so that a slight knock does not cause them to collapse. Throw the fabric loosely over the boxes, and fix with drawing pins where necessary, to stabilise. Use as shown above.

Mobile display

Age range
Three to twelve.

Group size
Individuals, groups or whole class.

What you need
Thin wire (eg florists' wire or wire coathangers), fine cord or nylon, painting and drawing materials, drawing paper or thin card, pair of pliers. (Fishing tackle traces can also be adapted).

thread

wire

mobiles

What to do
When you are studying a topic such as 'water', 'pond life', 'fish', 'transport', 'ourselves', or 'homes', effective displays can be conjured up by converting some of the children's smaller drawings into mobiles. Mobiles of parts of the body are always a source of interest. Hanging flash cards can help spelling.

Bend the florists' wire or coat hanger to make a loop which can have cut-outs suspended from them. Build up several connecting wires to suspend from and balance the cut-outs on each side. Use different lengths of fine cord to hang the objects for greater effect.

3D display box

Age range
Five to eleven.

Group size
Groups or individuals.

What you need
Wire screw eye,
block of wood,
strong cardboard,
card or Plasticine
gum strip or sticky tape,
knitting needle or
stick (as central post).

What to do
Make an unusual suspended display. Cut and stick together six triangular compartments as shown. The children can design their own 3D models made of card or Plasticine to fit inside the compartments.

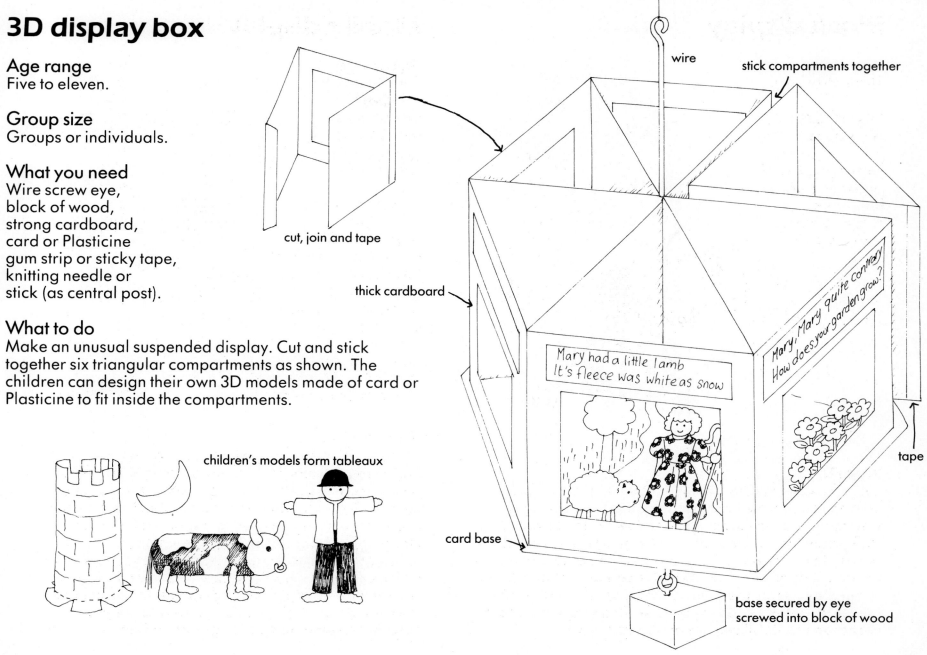

cut, join and tape

children's models form tableaux

wire

stick compartments together

thick cardboard

Mary had a little lamb
It's fleece was white as snow

Mary, Mary quite contrary
How does your garden grow?

tape

card base

base secured by eye
screwed into block of wood

Stained-glass windows

newspaper backing

Age range
Eight to twelve.

Group size
Large groups.

What you need
Tissue paper
(different-coloured sheets)
black paper,
glue,
windows to decorate,
newspapers,
scissors.

black paper→

coloured tissue paper→

glue

black strips of paper

What to do
Visit the local church to make studies of the stained glass
windows, the stories depicted and the colours used.
Make a simple window cut-out from black paper. Tear
strips and various shapes out of coloured tissue paper,
and arrange them on a newspaper laid on a flat surface.
Stick the window shape over the tissue paper and add
further thin strips of black paper to stick over the tissue
paper edges. Colourful abstract designs can be
produced fairly easily, as well as simple pictures.

Ideas for open days

Age range
Five to twelve.

Group size
Individuals
and small groups.

What you need
Large white
easy-stick labels,
thin card
lettering pens,
razor knife.

What to do
Arrange with groups of two and three children, and some
individual children who wish to work alone, that they will
select some piece of school work which they have
enjoyed to demonstrate to parents who visit the
classroom on open day.
   The children should work in pairs as 'facilitators',
meeting, greeting and taking the parents round as they
arrive as well as taking turns acting as demonstrators.
Hold a rehearsal on the previous day with all the class.

Set up tables with card labels. Cut a rectangle of the card and lightly score with a razor knife. Fold at the scoring so that the label will stand up on the table. Write on the label the activity under way.

Try to show a range of activities with the help of the demonstrators including:
- number,
- science,
- environmental/social studies,
- religious education,
- language,
- art work,
- craft design problem solving,
- computer education.

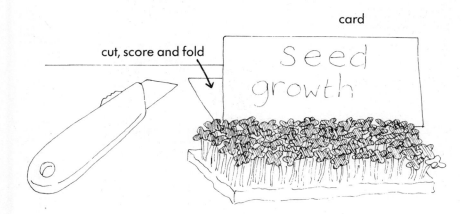

cut, score and fold

card

seed growth

demonstration of experiment

Each child should wear a name label.

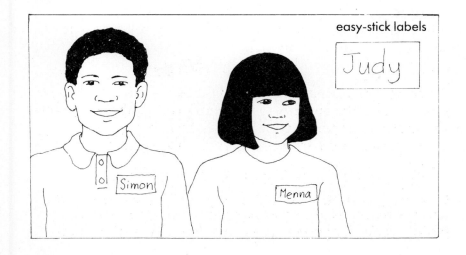

easy-stick labels

Judy

Simon

Menna

Theme displays

Age range
Seven to twelve.

Group size
Class or group.

What you need
Painting equipment, handicraft materials, display facilities.

CINDERELLA

What to do
A series of planning meetings should be held well in advance to agree with children and colleagues thematic displays for those special occasions when visitors are likely to be in school and need to see it at its best — open evenings, school plays or Christmas.

Each class works on paintings, 3D designs and collage on the special theme. If for example this was 'traditional pantomime stories', each class would select one fairy story to illustrate. A huge 'glass' slipper might be made in 3D, and coach and horses, princes, ugly sisters, Cinderella and Buttons could all be depicted.

Other classes might depict Aladdin, Puss-in-Boots, Mother Goose, Jack and the Beanstalk etc. The older children should be given the more technically difficult tasks, eg Cinderella with coach and horses. The younger children should be given the easier subjects such as Mother Goose and Jack and the Beanstalk. Other ideas for theme displays might include the following:
- Christmas carols.
- Easter scenes from the Bible.
- Christmas stories from the Bible.
- Special festivals of different faiths.

Favourite classics

Age range
Eight to twelve.

Group size
Class or individuals.

What you need
Thin card
rollers for paint,
tubes of lino-printing paint,
other painting materials,
laminated board or non-absorbent material,
newspapers,
razor knife,
letter stencils.

fold and score

Treasure Island

title

marbled paint

streamers

paintings

What to do
This display gives lots of opportunity for work on large scale collage and painting, but also on smaller scale activities such as producing different kinds of book covers, and work on lettering.

Squeeze lengths of two colours from the lino paints on to the laminated board: roll rapidly to mix. Roll the mixed paint on to the card 'covers' to produce an interesting marbling effect. When dry, paint the title on to the books using a letter stencil and white, black, or gold paint as appropriate. This looks very professional. Letters might also be stencilled on to paper and then cut out and stuck on.

The book cover can be displayed with paper streamers leading from it to key scenes.

Single book display

Age range
Five to twelve.

Group size
Small groups.

What you need
Books,
painting equipment,
display facilities.

What to do
Select a popular book for children, possibly something
which has also been on television; for younger children,
The Tale of Peter Rabbit for example, or for older
children *The Wind in the Willows*. Read the story to the
children, or with them, and draw up a list of good scenes
which they can try to illustrate. Produce ideas for each
scene to be depicted, and mount a display.

Top ten books display

Age group
Eight to twelve.

Group size
Class groups.

What you need
Books,
painting equipment,
display facilities.

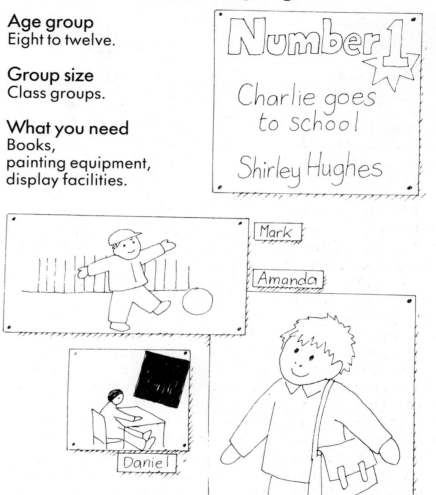

What to do
Organise a vote in each class for the best liked books.
Put the lists together to come up with the top ten and
arrange for each class to illustrate one book as before.

47

Temporary shelving

Age range
Three to twelve.

Group size
Large and small groups.

What you need
Folding clothes horse,
thick card,
string,
scissors.

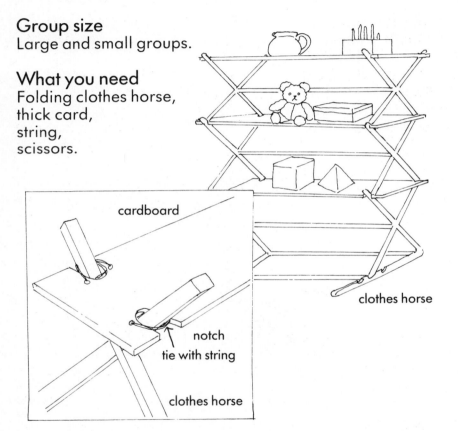

cardboard

notch
tie with string

clothes horse

clothes horse

What to do
Shelving is often required for temporary displays. Make
the shelves of card. Cut them slightly larger than
required, making notches where the struts of the horse
are. Make small holes with scissors in the card, and tie
them on to the horse with string.

Cheap free-standing display: 1

Age range
Three to twelve.

Group size
All groups.

What you need
Corrugated cardboard,
two chairs,
sticky tape,
stapler.

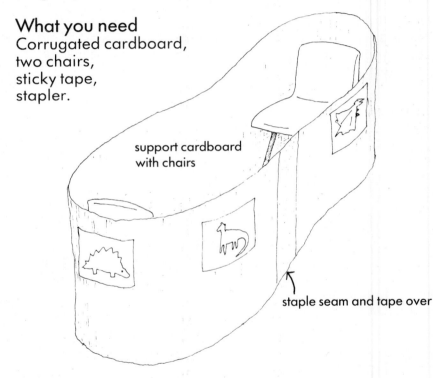

corrugated cardboard

support cardboard
with chairs

staple seam and tape over

What to do
Cut a large section of corrugated cardboard. Place two
chairs facing each other, and wrap the cardboard
around them. Staple at the seam, and overlay the seam
with tape if necessary. Pin the paintings etc to the
cardboard.

Cheap free-standing display: 2

Age range
Three to twelve.

Group size
All groups.

What you need
Cork or polystyrene tiles,
corrugated cardboard,
glue,
razor knife
or sharp knife,
stapler.

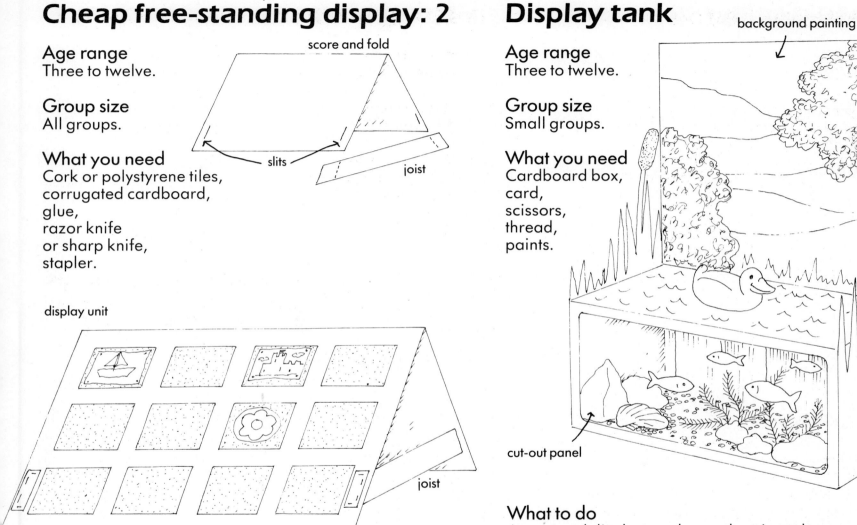

score and fold

slits

joist

display unit

joist

What to do
Make a prism shape from cardboard as shown. Cut slits
and insert cardboard joists for support. Cover the two
sides with cork or polystyrene tiles.

Display tank

Age range
Three to twelve.

Group size
Small groups.

What you need
Cardboard box,
card,
scissors,
thread,
paints.

background painting   wall

cut-out panel

shoe box

What to do
An unusual display can be made using a large
cardboard box or a shoe box. Cut out a panel from one
side and decorate the interior, hanging objects or
sticking them to the base to create a 3D panorama.
Decorate the exterior of the box too and place it against
a background wall painting.

Folding display

Age range
Three to eleven.

Group size
Any size
or individuals.

What you need
Stiff card,
scissors.

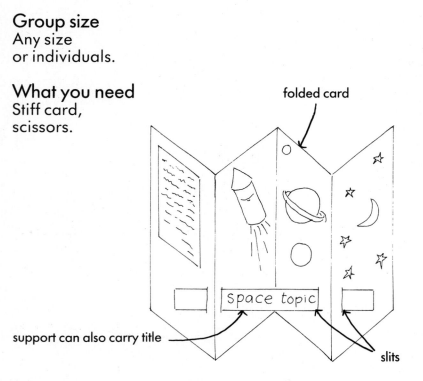

folded card

support can also carry title

space topic

slits

What to do
Make folds in the card to form a zig-zag shape. Cut slits in the folds at the front and thread a strong piece of card through. This has the effect of making the zig-zag shape firm and stable, less likely to fall over if put on display. The card threaded through can then be used to state the title of the topic. However if all the space is needed at the front of the card, the support can be threaded through at the back of the folds.

Using boxes as model displays

Age range
Three to twelve.

Group size
All groups.

What you need
A selection of cardboard boxes, stapler or glue, paper.

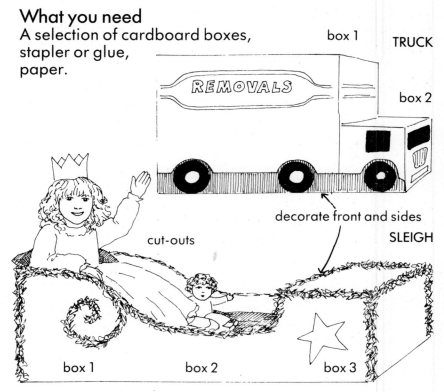

box 1   TRUCK

REMOVALS

box 2

decorate front and sides

cut-outs   SLEIGH

box 1   box 2   box 3

What to do
Stick or staple two or three boxes together, building different structures. Cut out the facing paper, and paint on, say, a truck, bus or sleigh. Attach it to the front of the set of boxes to give different effects.

Picture frames

Age range
All groups.

Group size
Individuals.

What you need
Shoe box with lid,
razor knife,
painting,
felt tips,
cord,
picture hook.

What to do
Simple frames can be made from a shoe box. Cut the box down to the dimensions of a shallow tray (1). Mount the picture inside this tray (2). Cut an aperture in the lid as shown (3); decorate the lid and refit it over the tray. Attach the cord to the frame, and hang (4).

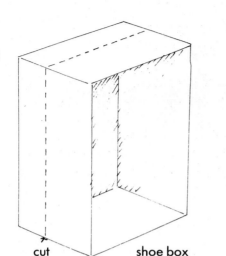

1

cut   shoe box

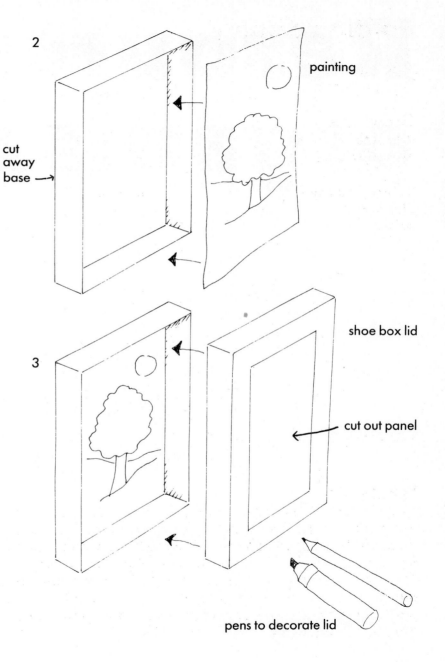

2

painting

cut
away
base →

shoe box lid

3

cut out panel

pens to decorate lid

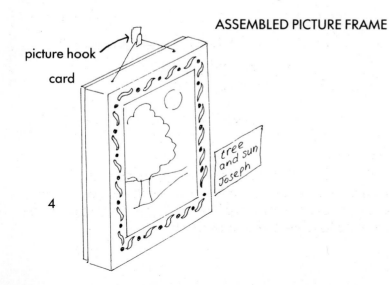

ASSEMBLED PICTURE FRAME

picture hook

card

tree and sun
Joseph

4

Resource organisation

Efficient organisation

Although resources are nearly always in short supply in primary schools it is surprising the amount of potentially useful bits and pieces that teachers collect. Educational authorities are likely to have central stores of furniture that has been replaced, renewed or unwanted. A visit to the store could result in a number of treasures being found. If items are stored correctly it is easy to devise systems for borrowing and lending.

Once you have established a labelled filing drawer with an alphabetical order, pairs of children can check the filing once a month. Similarly colour coded as well as labelled storage boxes can be checked by the children. They often find these sorting jobs quite therapeutic and feel they are important and are contributing something to the classwork. Instead of relying on monitors to distribute and collect materials train the children to be responsible for their own work and materials and generally tidying up. To prevent a stampede to the 'apparatus' or the book corner allow movement table by table.

When group work of different kinds is in progress site the resources for the different groups in different areas of the room. It is often very useful to have work ready on certain tables waiting for the children to come in so that they can start straight away.

Resource organisation is not only an efficient means to teaching, the way it is done or presented can inspire children and create a special atmosphere in the classroom – a strong motivation to work. Attractively displaying the work when it is completed will also encourage children to present and organise their own work well.

Establishing a clear understanding on how the classroom is run is to the benefit of all. Efficient organisation prevents the classroom from becoming cluttered, friction developing or accidents resulting.

Storing clay

Age range
Three to twelve.

Group size
Large or small groups.

What you need
Clay,
clay bins,
plastic sheeting
or cut up bin-liner,
large, deep, used
ice-cream container.

fill depression with water

ice-cream container

plastic sheeting

What to do
Most clay can be stored in bins which have tight fitting lids. However, it is better to spend a little time shaping the clay into smaller manageable pieces. Wrap them in bundles of five or six and cover them with plastic sheeting. This prevents the loss of a large lump of clay if the lid is inadvertently left slightly off by the children or the teacher. Large plastic ice-cream containers are ideal for storing enough clay for a small group of children. When the clay is put away for the day, the children can be encouraged to shape it into a circle, or cube etc. A small depression in the top of the shape can be made, and filled with water to keep the clay in a moist condition suitable for modelling.

Storing seeds and pins

Age range
Three to twelve.

Group size
Large or small groups.

What you need
Ice-cream containers,
coloured labels.

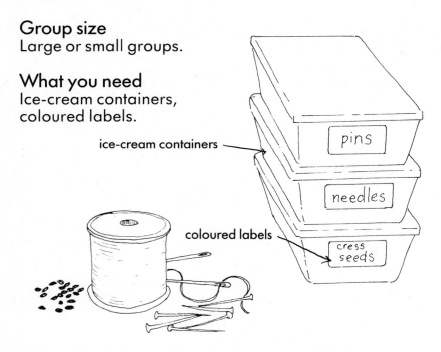

ice-cream containers

coloured labels

pins

needles

cress seeds

What to do
Large and small used ice-cream containers are very useful for storing items such as maths equipment, assorted seeds, and pins and needles. Put in the containers anything you want to be stored, and label accordingly. Use 'tacky-back' to affix labels, as these are easily removed when you want to change the contents. Make sure you use an appropriately coloured label to ensure that the box finds its way back on to the correct shelf; eg the blue label for the maths shelf, which you have lined with blue paper.

Handy storage packets

Age range
Three to twelve.

Group size
Large or small groups.

What you need
Pieces of pliable card,
stapler,
sticky tape
or tacky-back.

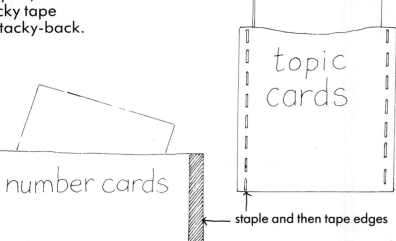

topic cards

number cards

staple and then tape edges

What to do
There are many occasions when you will need to store different-sized cards or large posters. Packets are easily made by folding card in half, to the appropriate size, and stapling the edges. Make sure that the edges are then sealed with either sticky tape or 'tacky-back', as staples can catch the skin if unsealed. Coloured tapes can be used to identify the type of packet within the colour code you have chosen.

Storing materials

Age range
Three to twelve.

Group size
Large or small groups.

What you need
Large plastic dustbin,
stacking vegetable
racks,
cutlery trays.

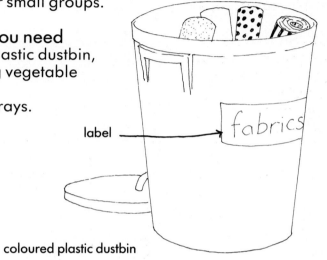

label

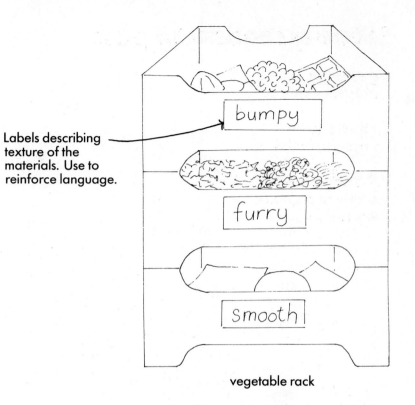

Labels describing
texture of the
materials. Use to
reinforce language.

bumpy

furry

smooth

vegetable rack

coloured plastic dustbin

fabrics

What to do
Larger materials can be stored and kept dry if put in
large coloured plastic dustbins. Older children can reach
in and help themselves. Small and younger children need
to be able to collect their materials from smaller stacking
stores, in which case vegetable racks are very useful.
Smaller pieces of materials can be sorted and stored in
cutlery trays, especially rods, strips, etc.

These containers, especially the vegetable racks, can
be labelled and colour-coded according to the language
work the teacher wants to encourage.

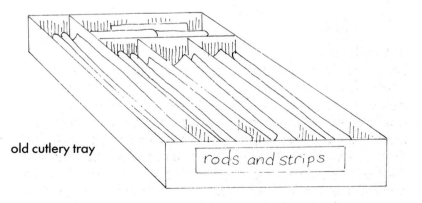

old cutlery tray

rods and strips

Storing solids

Age range
Three to twelve.

Group size
Large or small groups.

What you need
Medium-sized cardboard boxes,
shoe boxes,
roll of ready-pasted wallpaper
or greetings paper
(shops will often let you have
cheap end-of-line rolls,
and printers will
give you offcuts).

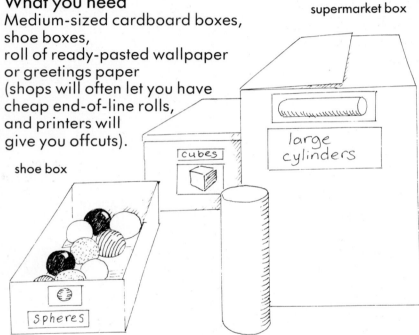

supermarket box

large cylinders

cubes

shoe box

spheres

What to do
Cover the cardboard boxes with paper. On the front of
each box stick a different solid shape: a cylinder, cube,
sphere etc. Labelling them will also help vocabulary and
spelling. Separate boxing-up reinforces the children's
concepts of solid shapes and also lets you see when a
particular shape needs replenishing.

Display workcard organiser

Age range
Three to eight.

Group size
All groups.

What you need
Sheet of card,
indexing cards,
ring binder,
felt tips,
picture scraps
or felt.

spiral bind

one   two   three

card

What to do
Use pieces of card and blank cards (obtainable from
educational catalogues) or cards which vary in size to fit
in a cataloguing box. You will need access to a machine
which spirally binds books. The variations of this idea are
limitless; one can use it for number, sentences, and
matching words or pictures. The teacher can adapt it to
his or her particular needs.

Decide on the format. Is it going to be number or a
matching activity, for example? Fold the card in half and
then put two small folds on either side of the centre fold
so that the card will be free standing when finished. Add
the cards as appropriate, and use felt tips, cut-up pictures
or felt cloth as desired. Remember to use non-fading felt
tips if the stand is to last for any length of time.

Protecting and storing workcards

Age range
Three to twelve.

Group size
All groups.

What you need
Photograph album sheets
with 'tacky-back' overlay,
prepared workcards
or other items to be protected.

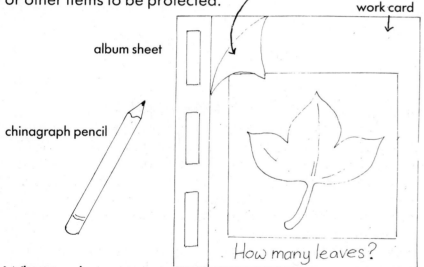

album sheet

chinagraph pencil

'tacky-back' overlay

work card

How many leaves?

What to do
Place the workcard inside the sheet of a photograph
album and put the 'tacky-back' overlay on top. You can
use these sheets with chinagraph pencils: this allows
writing to be rubbed off later so that the work sheet can
be used over and over again.

Book stands

Age range
Three to twelve.

Group size
All groups.

What you need
Cardboard boxes,
razor knife,
masking tape.

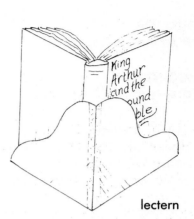

lectern

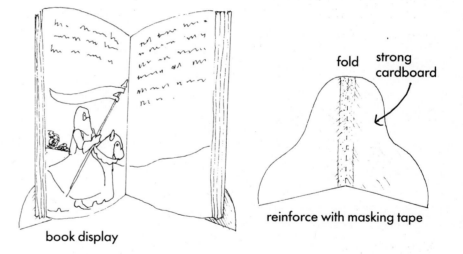

book display

fold

strong cardboard

reinforce with masking tape

What to do
A simple lectern for displaying books can be made from
strong cardboard boxes. Cut the cardboard to the
appropriate size and shape as shown. Seal the edges
with masking tape.

Water play

Age range
Three to seven.

Group size
Small groups.

What you need
Cheap plastic cups,
old metal knitting needle,
gas cooker.

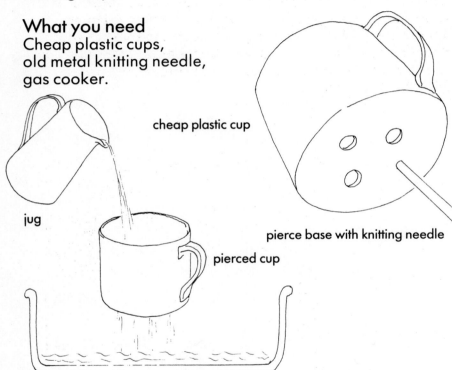

cheap plastic cup

jug

pierced cup

pierce base with knitting needle

What to do
Plastic cups with holes in are ideal for water play. Heat a
metal knitting needle in a gas flame and pierce the
bottom of a plastic cup with the heated needle. It is a
good idea to have six cups: in the first cup put one hole, in
the second cup two holes, and so on.

Reused cards

Age range
Three to eight.

Group size
Small groups.

What you need
White or coloured paper,
paper clips,
used Language Master cards.

clip on new word

topic
hat

old card

What to do
Sometimes one needs to recycle Language Master cards,
or perhaps use a different set of words temporarily, when
introducing a new topic. Cut an appropriately sized piece
of paper to fit over the used card, making sure not to
cover the recording tape. Fasten it with a paper clip. Re-
record the word to be used.

Ring binder word book

Age range
Five to nine.

Group size
Individuals.

What you need
Cards,
ring binder,
felt tips.

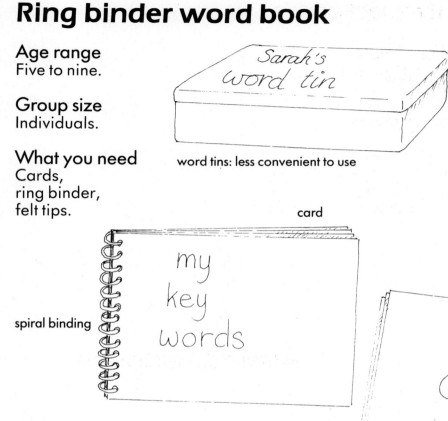

word tins: less convenient to use

card

spiral binding

my key words

What to do
As on page 56, you will need blank cards (obtainable from catalogues) or cards which vary in size to fit in a cataloguing box. You will also need access to a machine which spirally binds books. These machines can usually be found at teachers' centres or sometimes at larger schools which produce their own magazines. The machines are easy to use and are useful as an aid to making one's own books.

There are many variations to the uses of the ring binder wordbook. The idea that is illustrated is just one which can be adapted to individual children's needs. Teachers sometimes send words home in boxes, or word tins which can become muddled or lost. This method helps to keep the words together, and also allows the child to see the relevance of the words in a sentence. The key word is featured on its own on the left and used in a sentence on the right. For children who have difficulty with reading, it is always a good idea to use words that are relevant to the child. Using this method, personalised reading books can be created which the child will be more motivated to use.

key word

full sentence

go

We like to go to the shops

Storage and shape-coding

Age range
Three to twelve.

Group size
Class group.

What you need
Small strips of card,
sheet of larger card,
coloured sticky paper,
scissors,
adhesive
or stapler,
coloured felt tips,
'tacky-back'.

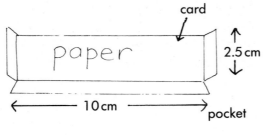

What to do
Cut small strips of card 2.5 × 10 cm and attach them in neat rows on three sides to the large sheet of card, so that you make small pockets. These pockets can be stapled or stuck with adhesive to the backing card. Cut out shapes and stick on the separate cards, which can then be put on the master code card. The shape-codes can then be recognised by the non-readers, with words written on the envelope for the readers. (If you have a Language Master then the word can be recorded on the strip of tape on the Language Master card.)

Use permanent felt tip for labels which are likely to be displayed for some time. Cover the display with 'tacky-back'.

When doing a project on shape, it is a good idea to use shape-coding as an alternative to colour-coding for some stored items.

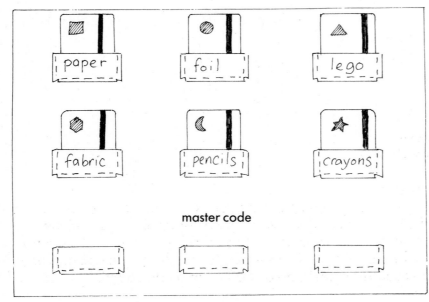

master code

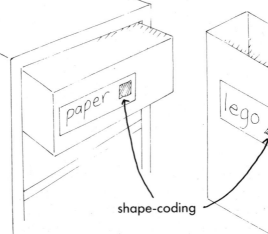

shape-coding

60

Teacher's tool kit

Age range
All groups.

Group size
Class group.

What you need
Plastic tool box.

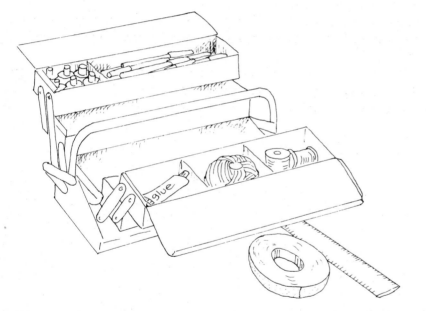

What to do
Fill your tool box with all the working equipment you possess: display pens, a ruler, scissors, glue, thread, needles, tape measure, tape, razor knife, pliers, marking pens, drawing pins, stapler, pins, string, sticky tape, paper clips. Check the pens and inks etc on a regular basis to make sure they are ready when you need them.

Handy storage drawers

Age range
All groups.

Group size
Class group.

What you need
Cabinet of small drawers
for nails, screws etc
(from any DIY shop).

DIY screw cabinet

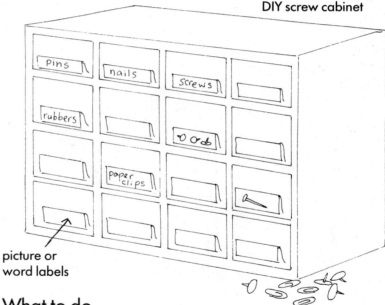

picture or
word labels

What to do
Store away supplies of pins, paper clips, nails, rubbers, drawing pins and so on in the drawers. Either label the drawers with words, for older children, or tape the items on the outside for younger children. Place the cabinet on the teacher's desk, on a shelf or in a cupboard.

Fun boxes

Age range
Three to eight.

Group size
Small groups
and individuals.

What you need
Large empty box,
coloured paper.

What to do
Large packing boxes can be converted into fun spots for
younger children. Close the box and lightly fix the lid. Cut
a large hole in one side, large enough for children to
climb in and out.

Baskets from boxes

Age range
Three to twelve.

Group size
All groups.

What you need
Shoe boxes,
razor knife,
stapler,
sticky tape,
crayons,
paints or
coloured paper,
paper fasteners.

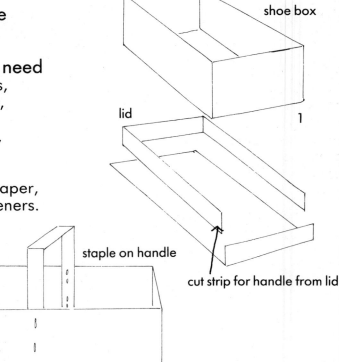

shoe box

lid

1

staple on handle

2

cut strip for handle from lid

What to do
Decorate the outside of old shoe boxes with crayons,
paints or coloured paper. Remove the strip from the lid as
shown in (1). Fix the strip with paper fasteners to form a
handle, and strengthen the corners with sticky tape.
Staple the handles for extra strength. The finished basket
(2) is just one of many useful classroom items which can
be made from shoe boxes.

A pair of scales

Age range
Five to eleven.

Group size
All groups.

What you need
Shoe box,
scissors,
knitting needle,
processed cheese box
or tin lids,
coins.

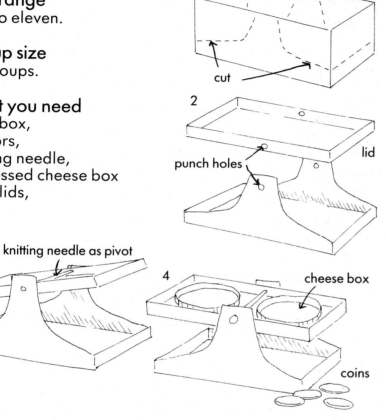

1 shoe box

cut

2 lid

punch holes

3 knitting needle as pivot

4 cheese box

coins

What to do
To make a pair of scales, find the halfway point and cut
the base of the shoe box (1). Punch holes in the side
supports and corresponding holes in the sides of the
upturned lid (2). Suspend the lid between the supports by
passing a knitting needle through the punched holes (3).
Tin lids, or the two halves of a cheese box, can then be
glued on to the lid (4). Coins can be used as weights.

Picnic boxes

Age range
Five to eleven.

Group size
All groups.

What you need
Cereal boxes,
sticky tape,
kitchen paper
or brightly coloured
wrapping paper,
glue, Marvin medium,
greaseproof paper bag,
string handles.

1 cereal box

tape   fold

2 wrapping paper

greaseproof paper
to line inside of box

3 handles

What to do
Cut a cereal box across the sides and the front, but leave
joined at the back. Fold across back and strengthen with
sticky tape to act as a hinge (1). Cover the outside with
kitchen paper and paint in bright colours, or cover with
wrapping paper. Each child can make a label with their
name on to put on the front of the box (2). To give the box
extra strength, paint over the outside with a solution of
Marvin medium and water, to give a strong shiny
exterior. Line each box with a greaseproof bag. To finish,
attach string handles to make it easier to carry (3).

Mixing palettes

Age range
Three to twelve.

Group size
Individuals and
class groups.

What you need
Plastic egg boxes
(the type with clear thin plastic),
or bun tins and trays,
sticky tape.

egg box

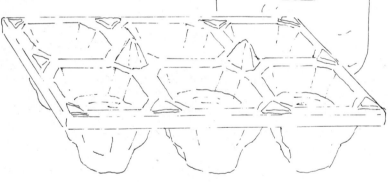

What to do
Cut the lid off the egg boxes, and place it on the bottom box. Tape the two halves together. Use for mixing rather than storage. The boxes also make useful powder paint reservoirs, since they are not too large. They also make useful temporary paste pots, but do not use them for glue.

Bun tins and cake trays will also make useful mixing palettes. Sheets of glass tend to be too dangerous.

Painting sponges

bath sponge

Age range
Three to five.

Group size
Large or small groups,
individuals.

What you need
Different types of sponge,
card,
stone,
stapler,
scissors,
elastic bands,
small scraps of material
and old tempera paint.

washing-up sponge

What to do
All kinds of sponge are useful for painting, from a cast-off bath sponge to the stick-sponge used for washing up. Sponges with bigger holes can be cut up easily with a pair of scissors. Cubes, wedges and cylinders are useful for painting or printing, either using a dabbing method or long exciting streaks. An interesting type of sponge is the layered foam that grapes come packed in. It can be found in most large supermarkets. This foam is around 1 cm thick and when cut into rectangles about 7 cm × 13 cm it can be stapled into a piece of folded card with an ordinary hand stapler. A piece of this foam 6 cm square, or larger, can be wrapped around a few scraps of material or a stone and secured with an elastic band. Being firm, these materials will make different sorts of marks in shape and texture. They can be used with powder or block paint as well as liquid.

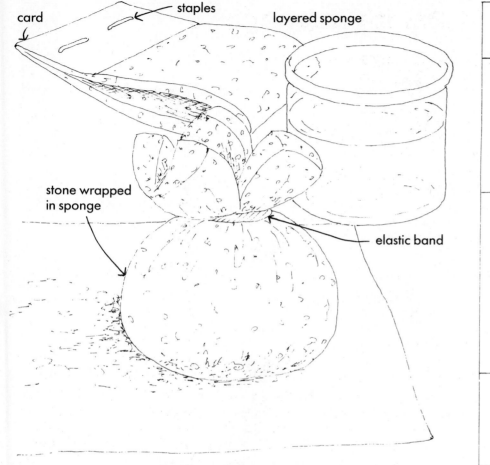

card — staples — layered sponge

stone wrapped in sponge

elastic band

SPONGE PAINTING

These squares can also be filled with scraps of block tempera paint scraped from the containers before new blocks are inserted. The sponges will then only need moistening in water before the child can produce pleasing effects which cannot be achieved with a brush.

Sponge activities are particularly important and valuable to the child who lacks control or confidence.

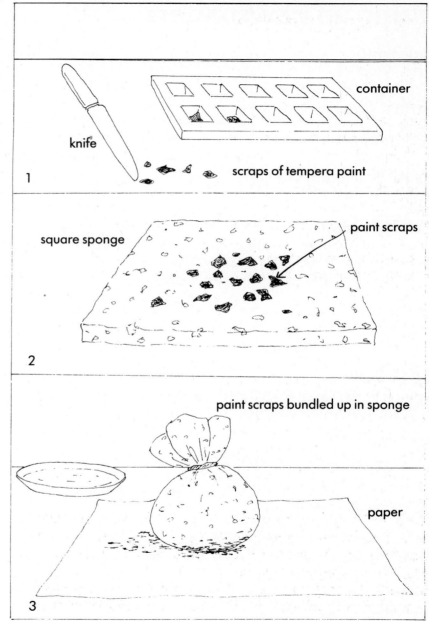

1
knife
container
scraps of tempera paint

2
square sponge
paint scraps

3
paint scraps bundled up in sponge
paper

Using up newspapers

Age range
Five to twelve.

Group size
Pairs
or individuals.

What you need
A pile of old newspapers, one for each pair of children.
Use papers of a standard size – all tabloids for example.
Count the pages so that all children have 30 pages of
newsprint. Give each pair a metre of sticky tape and a
pair of scissors. Paper, rulers and pencils may be
provided for other children as necessary.

What to do
Old newspapers are readily available and ideal for
small group problem solving. Ask the children to make a
house which will stand up on its own and be big enough
for one of them to sit in.

Suggest to older children that they try to design the
house on paper first. Give the children at least an hour to
do the task, and do not interrupt them or tell them what to
try. Let them settle to the task.

When the time is up hold an exhibition and run a 'test
trial' in which each house is entered and sat in.

Newspaper problems are useful for craft/design work
when you are running short of materials such as paper,
paints and egg boxes. Newspaper hats could be another
problem solving activity.

Guide-lines for successful designing
• Use the least amount of materials at minimum cost.
• Do the job successfully.
• Make the item look elegant or interesting.

Newspaper bridges

Age range
Seven to twelve.

Group size
Pairs and individuals.

What you need
Old tabloid newspapers,
a weight holder
set of weights (up to 1 kg)
ball of string,
reel of sticky tape,
card platform (5 × 5 cm)
to put over the bridge and
support the string and weights.

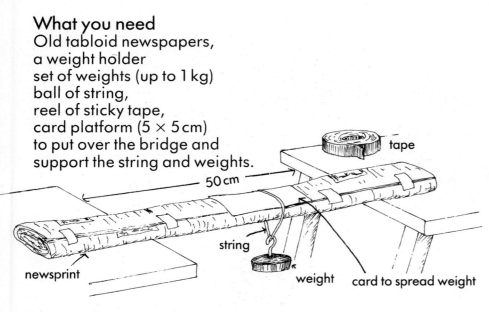

tape

50 cm

string

newsprint

weight   card to spread weight

What to do
Set the children the task of building a bridge between two
tables set 50 cm apart. They can use two sheets of
newspaper and 50 cm of sticky tape. The bridge must not
be attached to the table. The best bridge is the one which
holds the heaviest weight at its midpoint.
   Other bridge problems might include the following:
1 Make the longest bridge possible;
2 Make the widest bridge possible;
3 Make each support a 30 g weight at the midpoint.

Storing magazines

Age range
Three to twelve.

Group size
Small groups
or class.

What you need
Used cereal packets,
sheets of wrapping paper
or thin ready-pasted wallpaper.

cut diagonally

cover cereal box with paper →

Child Education

MAGAZINE CONTAINER

What to do
An empty cereal packet can be used to store magazines,
large books and work cards. Cut a diagonal line down
the front of the packet to make it easy to see what is
stored in the container when you have finished. Cover the
packet with the wrapping paper: this has the effect of
strengthening the packet, and the colour will remind you
of the contents if you use a permanent colouring scheme:
eg mathematics colour code – blue.

Record keeping, marking and work flow

Keeping records

Teaching is not only concerned with organising the classroom, the resources and the children but also with curriculum development and implementation. It is not possible to plan for the next stages of work unless the teacher looks at and records the children's performances on tasks and activities which have already been set. Careful study and recording of a child's performance identifies difficulties and problems. Thoughtful, systematic and carefully planned records enable the teacher to modify the curriculum to counteract any problems. The records should be capable of providing some continuity throughout the children's schooling and be passed on from teacher to teacher or from school to school. Record keeping also ensures that children engage in and complete a full range of school tasks.

Good record keeping need not be time-consuming and cumbersome. If it is it will soon peter out. Records should be appropriate for the tasks in hand. For example if a child is experiencing difficulty with reading, *pages 102 and 103* will help to isolate the particular problem.

Records enable progress in the curriculum and workflow to be monitored. They easily highlight areas which have received little or too much attention and enable the pace of progress to be monitored and perhaps speeded up. Children should be encouraged to mark their own work and assess it where appropriate. The teacher should read what they write and comment on the strengths. Children learn best from being told what is good and what may be a way of improving it rather than receiving negative comments such as 'Could do better'. Try always to make a positive statement and a developmental point on each piece of work. It is easier for children to make progress when they know what to do. Otherwise they become confused, frustrated and unmotivated especially when they have tried and failed but do not know why.

Topic records

Age range
Three to twelve.

Group size
Class group.

What you need
Photocopies of the empty record sheet (*see page 125*), felt tips, thin card envelope file (to store the records) ring-binder file.

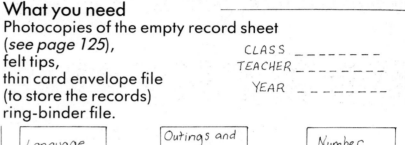

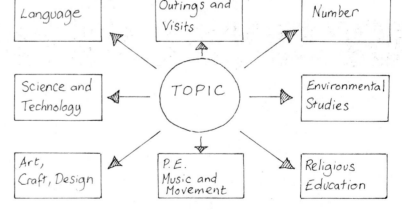

What to do
Fill in the empty spaces in the topic copy sheet on page 125. This will remind you of areas to deal with and plan for in a new topic. Keeping track of which class has covered which topic can provide useful information for each year. If a simple record is kept, a useful resource bank can be built up over the years.

Boxes for records and ideas

Age range
Three to twelve.

Group size
Individuals
and class groups.

FILING CABINET
WITH DRAWERS

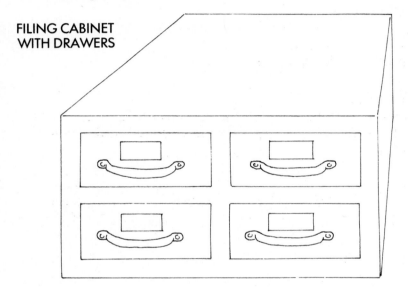

What you need
A set of filing drawers in a small cabinet, to hold 15 ×
10 cm cards, can often be bought at second-hand sales. A
much cheaper alternative is to buy small boxes of thick
plastic or cardboard with lids to house the cards. Some of
these box sets also contain a set of alphabetically
indexed dividers. You can also make your own small
boxes for the cards with a standard pattern. You will
need thick cardboard, scissors, adhesive fabric tape,
sheets of gummed paper and masking tape.

What to do
Cut the thick card to the dimensions shown below (1).
Score the outside of the box lightly along the dotted lines
as shown, and fold along the score marks (2). Secure all
edges with masking tape inside and outside for added
strength (3). Cover the box with sticky paper. Make a lid
and attach it to the box with a double lining of adhesive
fabric tape (4).

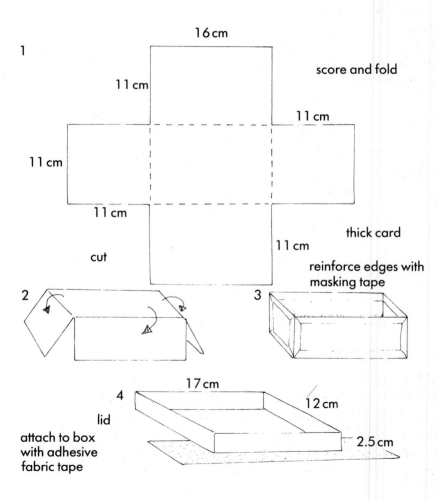

Language boxes

Age range
Three to eight.

Group size
Small groups.

What you need
Box,
set of 10 × 15 cm cards
(from a stationer's,
or make your own).

What to do
Keep a record of language games and materials, and spelling games and rules, on the cards. Sort into alphabetical order. You might, for example, file cards under 'silent e rule'; 'phonic games'; 'word games', etc. Devise your own system.

Number boxes

Age range
Three to eight.

Group size
Small groups.

What you need
Box,
coloured 10 × 15 cm cards,
unlabelled card dividers.

What to do
Make up word cards with sets of sums and sets of problems on them. Grade them in order of difficulty in each section:

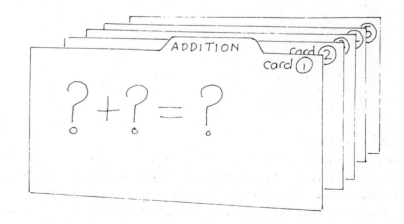

Grade from simple number bonds through to verbal problems in each section. These can be used to supplement published materials, or provide extension work for certain children.

Growth records

Age range
Three to twelve.

Group size
Individuals.

What you need
Metre rulers,
large sheets
of white paper,
coloured sticky paper
marked into 10 cm units.

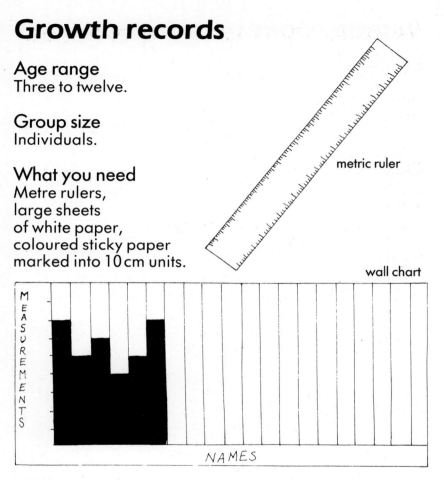

metric ruler

wall chart

MEASUREMENTS

NAMES

What to do
Each child's height is recorded on a chart, which they can complete using 10 cm units. On your separate record sheet (*see page 98*) record the child's height. Add to this record at a regular point in each term. Pass the records on to the next class teacher and the next school as the children move up. Over a period of time children's growth may take place steadily or in spurts; it should not stop altogether. Take advice if you are concerned.

Reading records

Age range
Three to eight.

Group size
Individuals.

What you need
Photocopies of checklist
(*see page 103*).

What to do
Listen to each child read from his or her book for a short period each day until they achieve fluency. Sit quietly by the child in a companionable, encouraging manner and listen to them reading. Move to a quiet area if necessary. Do not summon them out to your desk to stand and read to you. Help them relax.

Ask questions, to check that they have understood what they read. Fill in a checklist; turn to page 103 for a copiable inventory. Help from a specialist teacher may be sought for those of your children who you feel need additional help with their reading. Ask the teacher to fill in the informal reading inventory for you when she or he hears the child reading, so that you can discuss how to help the child together.

children's own records

Name _ _ _ _ _ _ _ _ _ _ _
has read these books during _ _ _ _ _

Title _ _ _ _ _ _ _ _ _ _
by _ _ _ _ _ _ _ _

Title _ _ _ _ _ _ _ _ _
by _ _ _ _ _ _ _

Title _ _ _ _ _ _ _
by _ _ _ _ _

Title _ _ _ _ _
by _ _ _ _

ring-binder

Record sheets may also be filled in by each individual child in the 6–12 age group. You will need ring-binder folders to hold the sheets so that the children may consult them. Ask each child who has completed reading a book to fill in their own record sheet (*see page 108*).

Reading and spelling progress records

Age range
Seven to twelve.

Group size
Class group.

What you need
Standardised spelling and reading text (suitable for the age group), photocopy of page 102.

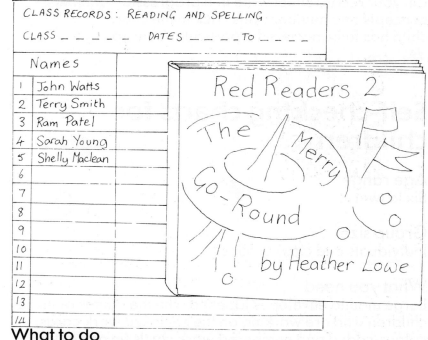

CLASS RECORDS : READING AND SPELLING

CLASS _ _ _ / _ _ _   DATES _ _ _ _ TO _ _ _ _ _

	Names	
1	John Watts	
2	Terry Smith	
3	Ram Patel	
4	Sarah Young	
5	Shelly Maclean	
6		
7		
8		
9		
10		
11		
12		
13		
14		

Red Readers 2
The Merry Go-Round
by Heather Lowe

What to do
Record results of tests on a photocopy of page 102, leaving at least six months between tests.

Number records

Age range
Three to twelve.

Group size
Individuals and
class groups.

What you need
Record sheet.

What to do
On your record sheet write in a progression of number
concepts and number skills. Tick in the chart when the
child has fully mastered a particular concept or skill.

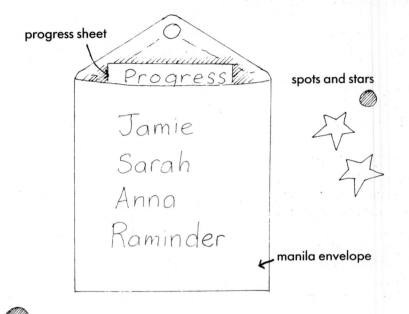

Self-checking charts for children

Age range
Six to twelve.

Group size
Individuals and class groups.

What you need
Large manila envelopes labelled with the names of those
children who are working on the enclosed work cards;
colour-coded and numbered work cards (in any of the
areas of the curriculum desired); thin card (same colour
as work sheets); glue; small red dots; 'easy' stick.

What to do
Stick a copy of a progress sheet on to the thin coloured
card, leaving a small coloured border round the chart. As
the children complete their numbered work cards they
collect a red dot from the teacher and stick it on their part
of the chart.

   It is surprising how even much older children find the
accumulation of the rows of dots very motivating and
satisfying. If wished, a silver star can be awarded when a
whole line is complete in the required or negotiated time.
This can also signify a team or house point. Progress
charts should be kept fairly private, and confined to small
groups or individuals to prevent too much competition.

My story book

Age range
Five to eight.

Group size
Individuals
and all groups.

What you need
Thick card,
coloured masking tape,
large sheets of paper,
string,
long-arm stapler,
thick strips of cloth,
adhesive,
wallpaper offcuts.

What to do
Personalised story books provide strong motivation when writing. Fold several large sheets of paper in half and fix them at the folded edge with a long-arm stapler (1). These will form the pages of the book. Cut card to make two covers, slightly larger than the pages of the book. Cut a further strip of card about 1.5 cm wide and as long as the two covers.

Cut a strip of the cloth to stick to the card, and glue it completely around the card on both the outside and the inside (2). Use string to tie the writing pages into the book cover (3) and also to suspend the book for display if so required. Bind the edges of the covers with coloured masking tape, in order to strengthen it. The cardboard might also be covered with offcuts of old wallpaper, to give a more professional effect. Label the front of the book, for example, '*My Story Book*' by Anna Miller; '*The Witch's Hat*' by Tom O'Reilly (4). The inside of the book can contain the children's own story, with his or her illustrations. Alternatively, it might feature a series of cut-out pictures which are used as the basis for a story.

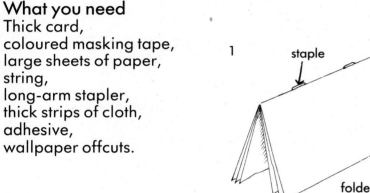

1   staple   folded paper

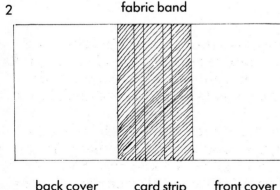

2   fabric band

back cover   card strip   front cover

3   bind in with string

4   string for display   My Story Book   by Anna Miller   masking tape

Plotting the plot

Age range
Three to eight.

Group size
Individuals or
class groups.

What you need
Children's work,
writings,
paintings, etc,
prepared background.

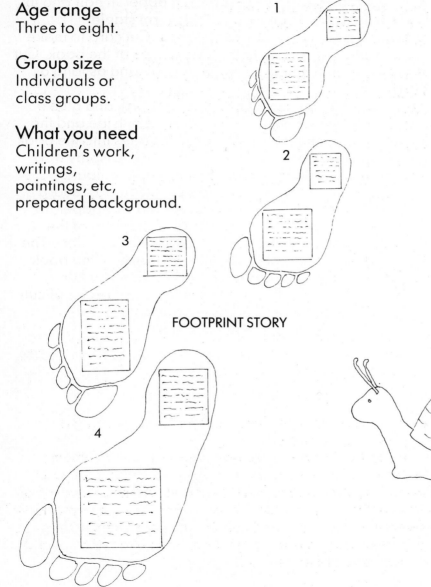

FOOTPRINT STORY

What to do
To stimulate young children to talk about what they see, it is sometimes valuable to present their work in novel and interesting forms. This can be done in a variety of ways. Here are two ideas:

• The story of a journey on a footprint made from drawing round prints of children's own feet. If the feet are made to gradually grow larger or smaller this gives the effect of coming towards or going away and can be used depending on the stories shown.

Footprints can be used to give the sequence of events in a single story to show how stories are made:

Character one	footprint one
Character two	footprint two
Place description	footprint three
First event	footprint four
Second event	footprint five
What characters do	footprint six
What results	footprint seven

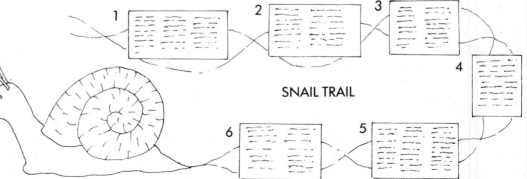

SNAIL TRAIL

• A snail with a story as its trail, or alternatively, observations of snails on the trail such as: What they prefer to eat; how they move (look at them through glass); colours and body and shell shape.

Marking and encouraging progress

Age range
Six to twelve.

Group size
Individuals.

What to do
Develop a range of techniques which the children can learn, which indicate to them how much personal progress they are making. The usual items are ticks and crosses and marks out of 10 which are found by counting up. Giving 8 or 9 out of 10 for imaginative writing is more dubious since it is difficult to be so absolutely precise. If you do use marks for story writing, explain how it was achieved, what was lost, what was missing.

Teachers often use grade words to mark work, eg very good, A; good, B; satisfactory, C; poor (not so good), D; very poor (not at all your usual standard), E. Put this scale up on the wall so that the children know how much they have achieved in comparison with previous grades. For younger children (five to seven) and non readers use a smiling face to show good work and talk to them about it.

It is always more encouraging to say 'Very good, Juan', than just 'Very good'. It is more encouraging to say 'Not so good as your last piece of work, Juan' rather than 'Very poor': that is negative. Try to explain how and why work is good, or what might make it even better. Then children know what to aim for.

Consider an example of the way in which meaningful comments can encourage writing development:

Denise is eight years old with a handwriting and reading and spelling problem, but with average intelligence. Comments which might be spoken or written would be: 'Very good, Denise; I like the way your short little sentences at the beginning build up the fear'; or perhaps 'This is just like a dream where it jumps from one thing to another suddenly. Well done!', or, 'Good story Denise. We must practise the spelling of *dream* together'. 'Well done, Denise' or 'Interesting story, Denise', or 'Good try', are not meaningful comments in so far as they encourage without trying to say *what* they are encouraging.

The teacher's smiling face and his or her attention are great motivators for children. Try to find more to smile at

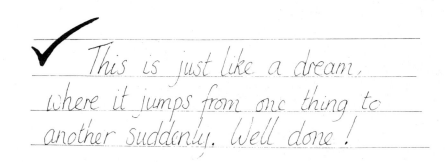

than to frown at. The classroom will then become a happier and busier place.

Try to avoid setting up 'payment by results' systems, which is bribery. Approval, and the sense of a job well done, should come to have their own intrinsic rewards or satisfaction. Try to wean children from stars and marks or sweets, to approval and constructive comment where you can. A special reward might be time to choose a special activity or story to be read.

Classroom behaviour

Guidelines for the classroom

Developing good relationships in the classroom is a most important factor in helping children learn, and in making teaching more effective. If children are made unhappy in school by their peers or the teacher, it will affect their progress in the curriculum. If they are fearful or anxious, their minds will concentrate upon their fears rather than upon the skills and concepts they should be learning. Whilst structure, order and discipline are important, these should not be applied so rigidly or harshly that elements of oppression, aggression and unfairness become apparent or are felt by the children.

The most effective climate for learning is found in a classroom where the teacher is firm, but kindly and supportive, where children are not ridiculed and bullied into submission or resentful silence. Quite often, some children are harshly treated in this way at home, so that before they can fit into the classroom routine they have to learn not to bully and hit out at the least provocation. They have to be taught to share with others and to help and encourage them. They have to learn to allow others

to receive attention and praise for good work, whilst they wait for their turn. Children learn to be negative if they are negatively treated. When they are positively treated, they learn to become positive.

If the teacher provides a good model of support, even for a troublesome child, this experience will be helpful to him or her and eventually will enable the vast majority of difficult children to settle. Only occasionally will it be necessary for some children to be placed in a smaller class group, whilst they learn to adjust their behaviour to the social setting in which the other children share and have opportunities.

Fostering valuable relationships and atmosphere is best done by the teacher, who should always seek to find the child doing something good – good work, making helpful suggestions, trying hard, helping others, or sitting quietly ready to begin. Try to make a positive comment on children's behaviour, rather than only giving them full attention when they are off-task or being a nuisance. This does not mean that you should completely ignore bad behaviour. You should stop it quickly, but without

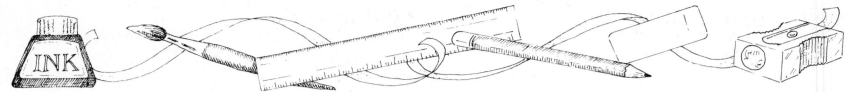

nagging. Try to find even more opportunities to praise children. However surprising it may seem, the most badly behaved children are the ones who feel worthless in their own eyes. This has arisen through their failure to gain their parents' love and support at home, or at school their failure to gain the teacher's esteem by easily learning to copy, trace, draw, read or write.

Such failures make them feel helpless and hopeless, and inferior. Some children will respond by withdrawing and becoming depressed; others will act out frustration at their lack of progress by clowning or disrupting lessons. It is often difficult to see these children as having low esteem: people who do not understand will often call them 'lazy' and 'unmotivated' or 'disruptive'.

If you can genuinely praise them for something and gradually show that you have respect and esteem for them, that they are not total failures or 'write-offs', and demonstrate that you can help them succeed, you will find that the misdemeanours in your lessons will diminish. Success in one area will gradually spread to other areas. Other staff will notice improvement in behaviour, and their positive response will help encourage it. The principle advocated is 'Catch them being good' ('C.B.G.') to build their self-esteem.

One of the other major principles of children's learning development is that they should be educated to become autonomous learners, able eventually to self-generate, to discover, to pose and solve problems. The teacher's management strategies should therefore be geared not to making the children dependent on the teacher for every decision, but able to weigh up what they need for themselves. They should learn to have a go themselves before rushing immediately for teacher's help. This will range from trying to put on their own shoes in nursery class, to guessing words from initial letter sounds when reading in reception class, to trying to spell a difficult word and looking it up in the dictionary before seeking teachers' help in junior school. To do each of these things, children have first to be shown how to make a start at any of these developmental tasks, and then shown how to build towards completion from that point. Some children will need to be shown only once. Other children will need to be shown repeatedly, and some will have to have the task broken into much simpler and graded steps before they can make progress.

Developing a supportive classroom climate, where failures are something which can be used as learning experiences and nobody minds having a go or perhaps not entirely succeeding, is one important side of the coin. The other is using these experiences and support to encourage in a learner a sense of self-worth and personal achievement. Each child should feel that he or she is a valued member of the group.

'Children are what they learn': if they are kindly and justly treated, they can learn to be kind and just to others. Children who feel supported, and have a sense of being valued for their abilities and contributions, can value others and feel free to think. They can experiment with ideas, hypothesise and solve problems in an independent manner. Anxious, dependent children seek order and sameness and the answer which teacher wants them to give: they are thus 'schooled' rather than educated.

Coming and going

Age range
Three to six.

Group size
Individuals and class groups.

What you need
A brief time at the beginning and end of the day.

What to do
Meet and greet all the children as they arrive with their parents first thing in the morning. Make sure each child has a few moments to tell you important things which have happened; games and apparatus should already be out or accessible, so that they can settle happily before the parent leaves. Reserve a few minutes at the end of the day after the story or work session, to tidy up and collect coats. Say goodbyes calmly and pleasantly. Try not to let the children rush off in all directions, late or in a hurry. Children rushing out of school can become careless, and forget to check oncoming traffic.

Lining up

Age range
Six to thirteen.

Group size
Whole class.

What you need
A brief time at the beginning and end of a lesson or work period.

What to do
Encourage children to come into the classroom and leave it in an orderly and calm quiet manner. Bring them in yourself. If the class is a boisterous, noisy one, make them line up outside the classroom and walk in quietly to stand at their places. They should wait for you to invite them to sit down. As they become calmer, they can be encouraged to come in, sit down and get out their work. In an integrated setting, they can settle down straight away to their own work. At the end of the morning, day or lesson, when they move out of the room, wait until they have put away their work tidily and returned to sit at their tables quietly before you dismiss them.

Dismissing

Age range
Three to six.

Group size
Class group.

What to do
Very often the children will be sitting on the mat listening to a story before they go home, or to lunch. Say: 'Watch me carefully and do what I do' or say: 'Show me who is ready!' Young children most often respond to this by sitting up straight and keeping quiet. To those who are quietest say 'Good Sarah. Good Leon. You can fetch your coats' and so on. As they return with their coats, say 'Come back quietly' and 'Well done'. Use this and other forms of praise to each child who remembers to come back quietly.

Alternatively, ask the children to sit quietly and 'with eyes closed'. When they feel a touch on their arm or hand, they can get up and fetch their coat. Anyone who peeps loses their turn.

Signing (younger children)

Age range
Four to seven.

Group size
Class group.

What to do
Before the group work begins, ask younger children to suggest signals which might be used to ask for quiet, eg hands raised; one hand or two; a finger on the lips; arm(s) raised fully extended; standing up etc. Vote on each one to find which is preferred.

Explain that when any member of the small group or larger class wants quiet to think or speak, all they have to do is, for example, raise their arm to signal that they wish for quiet. Other children seeing the signal must be quiet and they raise their arm too, until all is quiet for the speaker. Young children enjoy sharing control of the group in this way and become very responsive to each others' needs.

Signing (older children)

Age range
Eight to thirteen.

Group size
Class group.

What you need
Paper
or thin card,
coloured pencils
or felt tips.

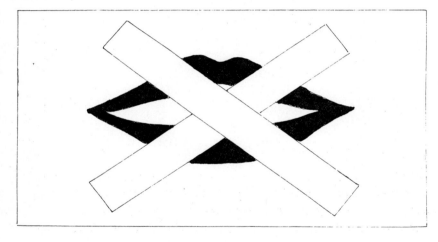

What to do
Before group work begins, ask older children to suggest signs which they might choose to use to gain silence from the rest of the class. List the signs on the board and vote to find which is the most popular. Each child then designs their own card with the agreed sign on it. When they want quiet, they must raise their card. Others follow suit, and when all are quiet the first signer may speak.

Classroom control

Age range
Five to thirteen.

Group size
Class group.

What to do
When you want to gain the attention of the whole class, you can follow these steps:

Step one: Make an attention-gaining noise: all teachers use one or another, eg 'Right'; 'Now then'; 'Um'; 'Class 3'; clap your hands; tap the table with ruler etc. Most, but not all children will respond.

Step two: Give short verbal instruction: eg 'Put down your pens and listen'; 'Sit still and listen'; 'Listen quietly'; 'Everybody be quiet please'; 'Class 3, be quiet'. Most children will be quiet, but a few will continue to talk quietly to each other.

Step three: Quietly name the children still talking: eg 'Samantha stop talking please'; 'Stephen,' etc. Naming can be done quietly because you always hear your own name in the noisiest room. Immediately the children fall quiet, start your lesson to gain and hold their attention.

As an alternative, when children are used to you, simply stand and wait for them to settle and be quiet. If they respect you, they will quieten. If they do not, you have further work to do.

Maintaining quiet

Age range
Three to thirteen.

Group size
Individuals and class groups.

What to do
Sometimes during work sessions the noise level rises too
high. Look round the room to locate the high noise area
and name one of the children in the group. Gesture to
him or her to quieten down. Whatever you are doing
have your ears tuned in to the rest of the class so you will
be quick to notice noise rising and can act well before
you have to shout for quiet. *The noisier you are the noisier
the children will become.*

Cueing

Age range
Three to thirteen.

Group size
Individuals within class.

What to do
When you think the noise level is beginning to rise, and
not to be about work, instead of calling everybody to
attention and disturbing those who are working, try:

Auditory cueing to individuals:
- a light cough,
- a tap on the desk with pencil,
- a snap of the fingers,
- quietly naming the child.

Visual cueing to individuals:
- eye contact,
- eye contact and a raised eyebrow or frown,
- the 'stink look',
- a shake of the head,
- pointing with the finger,
- a calming gesture with the hand.

This is often called '*lighthousing*' where to the child the
teacher's eyes appear to be flashing all round the room,
all seeing and all knowing.

Proximity and contact cueing to individuals:
- a calming hand on the shoulder,
- walking towards them,
- proximity – moving towards them and standing near,
- removing object of distraction,
- placing a calming hand on top of the head.

Pausing for attention

Age range
Three to thirteen.

Group size
Individuals within class.

What to do
When children start to talk or misbehave during stories or explanations, try pausing in the story and looking at the child or making eye contact. If the child becomes still and quiet, simply resume the story-telling. This avoids the need to nag and so spoil the story for the rest of the children. Try also quietly naming the inattentive child if she or he does not settle. Make eye contact and resume the story. With older children, break off in the middle of an explanation. Smile, and say: 'and Goldilocks said to the three bears . . .?' Direct it at the inattentive child. All the others will laugh or smile and look at him or her. Not quite understanding what is going on, he or she will quickly realise they are the focus of attention and try to find out why.

   Instead of reprimanding children who are inattentive, ask them a question about the story or the talk. This will gain their attention and keep that of the other children. If they cannot answer, ask another child to help them out, and praise them for doing so.

Catch them being good!

Age range
Three to thirteen.

Group size
Individuals, groups or whole class.

What to do
Whenever children are *on task*, and doing as they are told and working, or trying to do so, praise them and smile at them. This will encourage them to work harder. They will feel significant because they have been noticed and appreciated. Too often it appears that children are only caught when they are actually misbehaving, or about to, and they are then nagged. Try to reverse this process and 'catch them being good' ('C.B.G.') instead. This will be very hard with some children, but if you persevere you will eventually succeed. The change in some children's behaviour with 'C.B.G.' can be striking.

   Consider an example. If you want all the children in PE to make 'curved shapes', but one child does not join in and starts to misbehave, choose a child near to the talker or misbehaver and praise that child's performance. As soon as the misbehaver starts to make a curved shape, praise him or her, and offer as much encouragement as possible. Similarly, stop talkers by praising quiet children near them for behaving.

Attention grabbers

Age range
Three to eight.

Group size
Small groups and whole class.

What to do
Experiment with useful phrases for gaining the children's attention. Examples might be on the following lines:
'All show me your hands;'
'Show me your eyes – I want to see everyone's eyes looking at mine;'
'Show me ten fingers, six fingers . . .;'
'All children with lace up shoes . . .;'
'All children with fair hair . . .;'
'Tiptoe quietly to your table . . .;'
'Touch your elbows, touch your nose . . .;'
'Go sit on your chairs and rest your heads;'
'Close your eyes.'
Try to avoid saying 'girls' then 'boys line up', so that you do not encourage stereotypes.

Troublesome arrivals

Age range
Three to six.

Group size
Individuals or groups

What to do
If a young child is brought to school and is in tears, or starts to scream and yell when left, quickly show him or her something bright and colourful or noisy to distract attention and draw it towards the object. If you suspect the child is going to cry when left, try to engage him or her in some form of play before the parent or guardian leaves. As soon as the child is engrossed in play, it will be easy for the adult to leave. Some children (and parents) might need a period of weaning, during which the parent stays in the room, but disengaged from the child.

Engaging brains

Age range
Three to thirteen.

Group size
Individuals.

What to do
As soon as the children are busy working, move round and try to make some positive statement about the work each child is doing. Try to make them understand why some aspect of what they are doing is good, or how it will be good, or better than last time. Move round the class making positive 'brain-engaging' comments to every child during the session. You will be rewarded by finding they will concentrate and work harder for you.

Story comments

Age range
Seven to thirteen.

Group size
Individuals.

What to do
As you move round the class, ask the children to read their stories to you. In reading them aloud, they will notice their mistakes and will learn to 'self-correct'. Discuss elements of the story with each child, and offer praise and questions to extend the story skills. Leave each child with comments such as: 'Darren, two things to think about in your story. One, why did the boy open the parcel? Two, who was it addressed to?'

Discipline through work

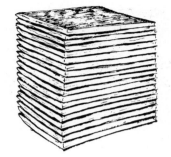

Age range
Five to thirteen.

Group size
Class, group or individuals.

What to do
When you find the children noisy check through the following list:

1 Was the task too difficult for most of them? This will make them noisy and frustrated, so that they become irritable or clown about.
2 Was the task too easy for most of them? Have many of them finished more quickly than you planned, and are now telling a good yarn?
3 Was there too much 'dead time' for the able and slow learners? If the range of tasks set was not sufficient the very able (14% of the class) will finish in about one-third to half the time of the average (72% of the class). This gives them a large span of 'dead' time.
   The slow learners (about 14%) set work for the average level will often work in a shallow way and finish within two or three lines: they too will have dead time on their hands, to fill with mischief.

Move around the class so that you can find out these children's needs and modify the work set accordingly. Plan ahead, and when preparing work, always try to think of extension work on principles and problems for the able, and of smaller more structured steps for the slower learners. In this way all of them will be kept busy and interested. If the children are interested in what they are doing they will become involved with the work and devote less time to talking to others and misbehaving.

Leading into the hall

Age range
Five to thirteen.

Group size
Class group.

What to do
Quietly line the children up at the classroom door. The noisy children will most often make up the rear section of the queue. Ask the front children to lead the whole class responsibly into the hall. Walk with the children two-thirds of the way back, so that you can see the front of the queue and control the back of it, the noisier ones. Do not remain behind in the classroom dealing with trivia, leaving the children to their own devices.

An alternative method is also effective. Line children up at the classroom door quietly. Lead the front of the queue out of the classroom towards the hall and at the corner or a critical point where you can see most of them – STOP! Allow the queue to file past you, so that you can make sure they are quiet and under control. Move forward again with the last third or the potentially most noisy section of the line.

Class control

Age range
Three to thirteen.

Group size
Individuals, groups or class.

What to do
Set the children to work. As soon as they settle down to work the noise level will go down. Any child who is not working but attention seeking will begin to become noisy.
1 Name the child quietly eg 'Stephen!'
2 The child will look at you or get on with work.
3 Three seconds later, the teacher must look back at Stephen to check that he really is still quiet, or not playing about again.
4 The eye contact will be enough to warn him that you are watching him.

Idle threats?

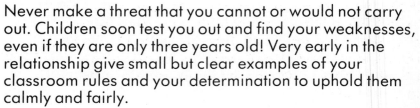

Age range
Three to thirteen.

Group size
Individuals, groups or class.

What to do
Never make a threat that you cannot or would not carry out. Children soon test you out and find your weaknesses, even if they are only three years old! Very early in the relationship give small but clear examples of your classroom rules and your determination to uphold them calmly and fairly.

Rules and how to keep them

Age range
Three to thirteen.

Group size
Individuals and class groups.

What to do
Have as few rules as possible. Ensure that the rules you do have are those which encourage reasonable behaviour and sociability: eg 'Do not run in the classroom'; 'Do not shout'; 'Do not tell tales'. Always explain the reason for the rules to the children. Involve older children in the making of rules. Remind them of the rules if they break them — and keep them yourself!

Queuing in class

Age range
Five to thirteen.

Group size
Whole class.

What to do
Try to move around the class looking at children's work and helping them, instead of allowing a queue to form round the teacher's desk. Once children form a queue they stop work altogether and chat. Even if you deal quickly with them, some children spend all lesson joining and re-joining the queue to avoid working. The queue often blocks the teacher's view of the rest of the class, allowing other misdemeanours to occur and the noise level to rise.

Calming down

Age range
Three to thirteen.

Group size
Individuals.

What to do
Move quietly to the shouting child and put a calming hand on the arm, shoulder or the top of the head, and very quietly say: 'Don't shout . . ., we are not deaf.' Say: 'Ssh ssh,' soothingly if the child continues. Make eye contact as you do this, and settle back to work. Keep an eye on the child for a little while in case of further upset. Children shout because they are excited, because they are angry, or because this is the typical mode of communication at home. Shouting makes it impossible to use long and complex sentences to communicate ideas, and so behaviour deteriorates.

Beware: when one child shouts, others imitate or shout louder to be heard. It is important that you do not get involved in this spiral, for the teacher provides a model which the children will imitate. Step in quickly and calm them down as indicated above. Do not do it negatively or harshly.

Sending out?

Age range
Three to thirteen.

Group size
Individuals.

What to do
Check the school's accepted procedures. Most schools' rules do not advise sending a child out of the room unattended. If you do, he or she may run away; run home; vandalise the cloakrooms; pull faces through the window; have an accident.

It is best not to send a child out of the room, but to send them to a quiet area or 'time out' region of your own room. If you must send him or her out, *first* send a responsible child to fetch the head or helper to escort the child, or leave the class with another teacher and escort the child yourself. Do not leave your class unattended.

Time out chair

Age range
Seven to thirteen.

Group size
Individuals.

What you need
A special chair.

What to do
When a child becomes upset or angry for any reason, and starts to shout, refusing to cool down, send him or her to sit on the 'time out' chair for 30 seconds. Do not treat this as a punishment, or as an old-fashioned dunce's stool — that would be cruel. The time out chair or cushion should simply be a neutral zone, for calming down and regaining composure. The time out set should be of very short duration: 10–30 seconds is usually sufficient for young children. At the end of the time period, they should be very quietly asked if they are ready to resume activities. They should not leave the chair unless invited to, or unless they quietly tell the teacher they are ready to do so.

The 'time out' chair can also be a 'refuge'. Children under stress, who wish to use the neutral 'time out' chair for a short period, should always be allowed to do so. It can be a signal for help, a means of avoiding another child's irritation, or a place to be quiet when you are upset. Whilst in 'time out' no-one should be allowed to speak to the individual, or attract his or her attention.

Occasionally the teacher may wish to use the 'time out' chair too, for a few moments' peace and quiet! 'Time out' is for calming and quietening, not for work.

Time out cushion

Age range
Three to six.

Group size
Individuals.

What you need
A large cushion.

What to do
Encourage very young children who are upset or irritable to go and lie down on a special cushion for 30 seconds to a minute, in order to calm down. Seriously upset or disturbed children can be left longer, perhaps even to sleep off their distress. Fluffy cushions should be provided for comfort, and peacefully coloured ones for a calming effect.

Behaviour 'contract'

Age range
Seven to thirteen.

Group size
Individuals.

What you need
Photocopy of page 104.

What to do
When a child's noisy, disruptive behaviour will not respond to 'C.B.G.', 'time out', or any other technique, as a last resort you can try 'behaviour contract'. Discuss the problem with the child when you have him or her alone. State what behaviour you will and will not accept. Explain why you think the behaviour is unreasonable and how it prevents other children from learning and benefiting from the discipline. Seek to gain a measure of understanding and co-operation from the child, and then draw up a simple 'contract' stating what behaviour the child should try to achieve. He or she can collect a tick or a signature at the end of an appropriate lesson period or time interval. This is very often enough to help the child understand the undesirable nature of bad behaviour. It helps if the parents can be involved, to support good behaviour and encourage the gaining of ticks and signatures.

Counselling

Age range
Three to thirteen.

Group size
Individuals.

What to do
When children, however old, persistently misbehave, try not to shout and make a fuss and so give attention to the bad behaviour. Instead, keep them behind at playtime or lunch time and quietly ask what the problem was, and what the fuss was about. Try to avoid face-to-face confrontation; sit beside the child and talk.

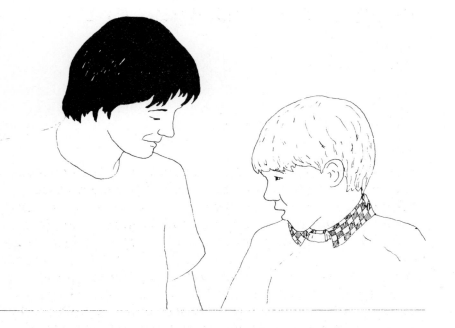

Targeting (irregular habit)

Age range
Seven to thirteen.

Group size
Individuals.

What you need
Pencil,
copy of page 101.

What to do
When a child misbehaves at irregular intervals, and you feel at a bit of a loss about what to do, watch the child closely to spot the least desirable behaviour (eg shouting or calling out). Simply record with tallies on the copy page 101 every time you see the unwanted behaviour occur.

Observational record		Date: Time:
Child:	Age:	Class:
Time of day	Type of misbehaviour	
9.00 – 10.00		
11.00 – 12.00		
lunch		
1.15 – 2.15		
2.15 – 3.15		

Targeting (regular habit)

Age range
Three to thirteen.

Group size
Individuals.

What you need
Pencil,
copy of page 100.

What to do
Record each time any unwanted or disruptive behaviour occurs by putting a tally mark on copy page 100. If the pattern appears to be relatively regular throughout the day (and with different teachers) you will find that the very act of recording will often cause the misbehaviour to cease. This is because you are noticing it as it occurs, but not making a fuss about it or giving it extra attention. If targeting does not work to any extent, try 'C.B.G.', then 'time out', and then 'behaviour contract'.

Setting the right atmosphere

Age range
Three to thirteen.

Group size
Individuals and whole class.

What to do
Adopt a positive and supportive style yourself. This will show the children how to behave to each other. If you nag and are bossy and irritable they will behave in a similar manner. If you are calm and kindly they will be too. Encourage all peer support behaviour and discourage tale-telling, scapegoating and unfriendly comment.

Progress encouragement

Age range
Three to thirteen.

Group size
Group and whole class.

What to do
Only encourage the children to compete with themselves – to improve on their previous work. If you encourage competition between children, only one can win – which means that some 31 others must fail. Failure engenders negative feelings and low self-esteem, especially in those who are always failing in comparison with their peers. In the end, those at the bottom of the heap give up trying and begin to evade work, or become disruptive to gain esteem in other ways. Any form of attention is better than none. Try to find something which each child is good at.

Reproducible material

Timetable

Times	Monday	Tuesday	Wednesday	Thursday	Friday
		LUNCH			
clubs/ meetings					

Diary dates

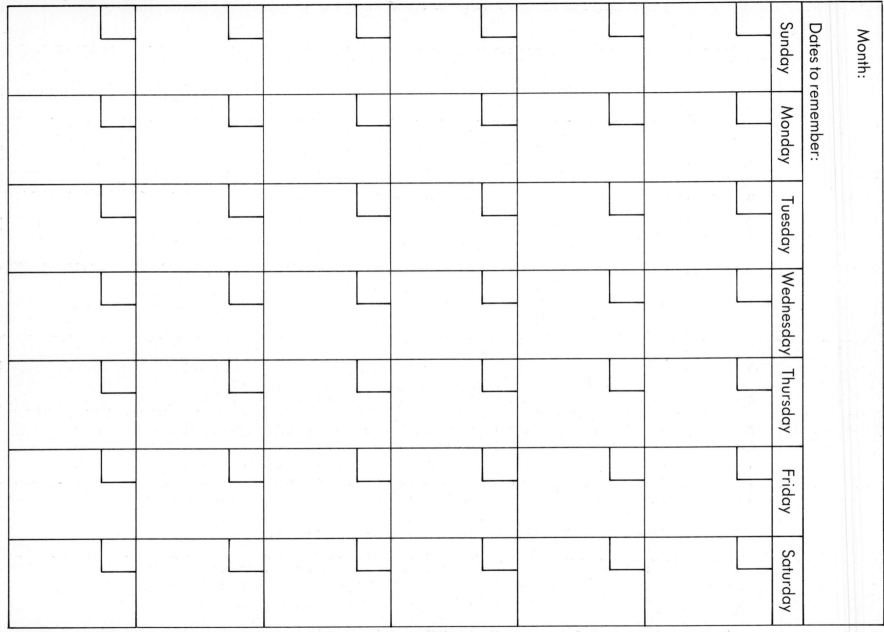

Dates to remember:	Sunday	Monday	Tuesday	Wednesday	Thursday	Friday	Saturday

Month:

Group records

	Name	

This page may be photocopied for use in the classroom and should not be declared in any return in respect of any photocopying licence.

Class records

Name	1	2	3	4	5	6	7	8	9	10	11	12	13	14	15	16	17	18	19	20	21	22	23	24	25	26	27	28	29	30

Stock list

Stock list							
Item	Orig No.	Date	Date	Date	Date	Date	Comment or Serial Number

Record sheet

Record sheet				
Target child:				
Date:				
Time of day	Observational record (what you saw child do)	Activity/Lesson	Tallies	

Observational record

Observational record

Date:
Time:

Child: Age: Class:

Time of day	Type of Misbehaviour								
9.00–10.00									
10.00–11.00									
11.00–12.00									
Lunch period									
1.15–2.15									
2.15–3.15									

Class records: reading and spelling

Class ___

19 ___ → 19 ___

Names	R. Age July	Test	S. Age July	Test	R. Age January	Test	S. Age January	Test	R. Age July	Test	S. Age July	Test
1.												
2.												
3.												
4.												
5.												
6.												
7.												
8.												
9.												
10.												
11.												
12.												
13.												
14.												
15.												
16.												
17.												
18.												
19.												
20.												
21.												
22.												
23.												
24.												
25.												
26.												
27.												
28.												
29.												
30.												
31.												
32.												

Class Teacher: ___

Hearing reading: monthly progress record

Name: _____
Class: _____ Date of Birth: _____
Reading Scheme: _____
Spelling Age: _____

AT TEST
Chronological Age: _____
Reading Age: _____
Reading Test: _____
Spelling Test: _____

Categories	Examples	month	month	month	month	month
TEXT	Book and page number. Criticism if any.					
WORD ATTACK SKILLS	Guesses from initial sound. Tries blend. Self corrects.					
COMPRE-HENSION SKILLS	Can answer factual recall questions. Can predict using picture etc.					
AUDIENCE EFFECTS	Pauses and drops voice at full stop. Reads in units of meaning. Speed.					
BEHAVIOURAL SIGNS	Reading position. Body posture. Finger or book mark used.					
EMOTIONAL SIGNS	Tenseness. Nervousness. Lack of fluency and monotone.					
OTHER COMMENTS	Select one thing to help with reading.					

Conclusions: _____

Post tests R.A. _____ S.A. _____
(at least 6 months later.)

Signature: _____ Date: _____

This page may be photocopied for use in the classroom and should not be declared in any return in respect of any photocopying licence.

Contract form

Contract

Name: _____

promises to

1 _____

2 _____

3 _____

4 _____

5 _____

on _____

My signature _____

Date _____

Teacher's signature _____

Date _____

Balloon 'contract'

Colour in each balloon when you have done each job it asks you to do.

I am going to

write

read

listen to

This contract was made by: _____

Started on: _____   Finished on: _____

Teacher's signature: _____   Date: _____

'Nudge' sheet

Nudge Sheet

How did it go?

Activity	I liked it . . .	It was O.K.	I did not like it

What did you like best? _____

What did you not like? _____

Topic report

My Topic

Name

1 Title of my topic

2 I will use some of the following for my research

☐ books   ☐ filmstrips
☐ newspapers   ☐ videos
☐ magazines   ☐ cassette tapes
☐ brochures   ☐ records
☐ computer   ☐ pictures
(tick the ones you will use)

3 When I have all my information on my topic, I will share
   it with others by:

☐ writing and illustrating my own book
☐ presenting a talk, using charts I have made
☐ recording on cassette a talk about the topic
☐ making posters to show what I have learnt
☐ making models of things I have been studying
☐ using overhead projector and a talk
☐ video film and a talk
☐ _____
(tick the one you will do)

4 When I have finished my topic I will write a
   page evaluation of my research, including the things I did
   well and the things I could have done better.

5 I will choose _____ special words I find during my research,
   list them with their meanings and learn to spell them.

Topic completed

Date _____   Signed _____

Comments _____

_____

_____

Reading list

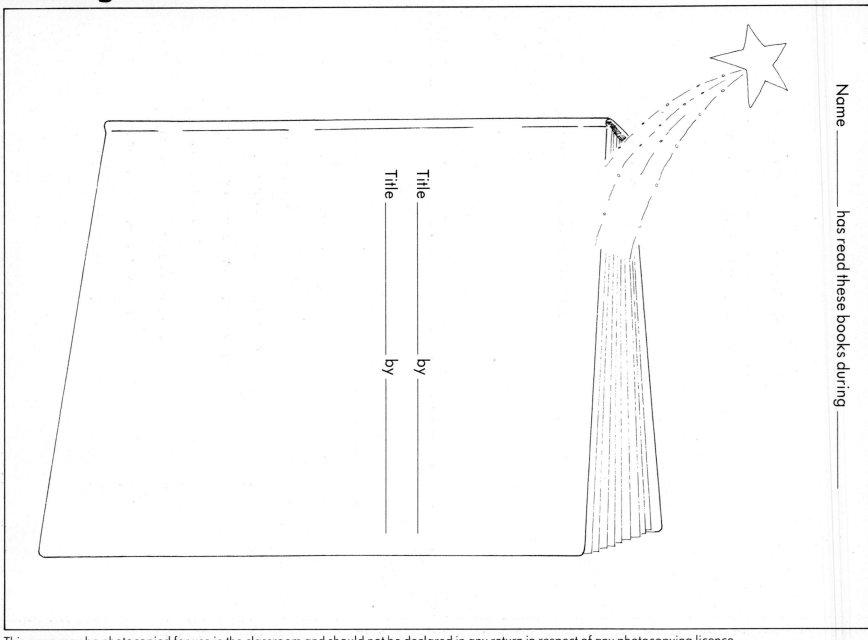

Title ——————— by ———————————————

Title ——————— by ——————

Name ——————— has read these books during ———————

Reaction cards

Card 1

How did things go today?

I understood the lesson ☐

I did some reading and writing ☐

I listened and joined in everything ☐

I finished most of my work ☐

I talked to the teacher about my work ☐

I am pleased with the work I did today ☐

I enjoyed the lesson today ☐

The part I enjoyed the most was ——— ☐

Card 2

Did you enjoy reading the book?
- Yes ☐
- No ☐

Did you find the book?
- Easy? ☐
- Difficult? ☐
- O.K.? ☐

What did you not like about the book? ———

Which was your favourite part? ———

Evaluation form

ACTIVITY

	AM PM	Checklist for equipment	Language
Date:			
Names:			
Adults:			
Children:			

Difficulties encountered

Evaluation

Memo note

To _____

Mr/Mrs/Ms _____

☐ telephoned ☐ called in ☐ wrote a note

to say _____

please ☐ telephone ☐ write a note
        ☐ make time to see

Message taken by _____

Date _____ Time _____

Request for materials

Dear Parent,

For a class activity on _____
it will help us greatly to have the following items:

_____

If you can help please arrange for the items to be at school on _____

Thank you.

Signed _____

Class outing letter

Dear Parent,

We are planning a visit to _____

Departure will be at _____ on _____

Cost will be _____ for each child.

_____ will need _____

_____. We will arrive back at _____ approx.

If you would like your child to participate please complete the form below and return it to school by _____.

Signed _____   Date _____

✂ -

CONSENT FORM

I would like my child to take part in the school visit to _____ on _____.

Signed _____   Date _____

Parent help letter

Dear Parent,

We need extra helpers in the classroom to assist in the following areas:

_____

_____

_____

We look forward to hearing from you, if you can help.

If you can spare _____ hours a _____, please fill in and return this form.

Date _____

Signed _____

✂ -

I should like to help, I will be available on

My special interests are: _____

_____

Date _____

Signed _____

Sports Day letter

School Sports Day

Dear Parent,

We are holding a school sports day on _____ at _____ if the weather is dry. You are most welcome to come and cheer on the competitors and join in the fun. There will also be several parents' events which you might like to enter.

Your child is entered for:

1 _____

2 _____

3 _____

We do hope you will be able to come.

Yours sincerely,

Class teacher

Paired or praised reading project

Community School – Parent Involvement Project

Dear Parent,

It has been found that if parents listen to their children read in a special way for a few minutes each day this helps the children learn faster.

If you would like to meet us and hear about how to do this please come on ———— at ———— for 20–30 minutes. Grandparents would be very welcome to come along too or in your place if you cannot be there.

Yours sincerely,

Class teacher

Tea and biscuits will be provided.

Class visits

School ——————   Date ——————

Class visit to ——————

Dear Parent,

As part of our project work on —————— we intend to visit —————— . We shall leave at —————— and arrive back at —————— . Please would you sign the form below to say whether or not you give permission for your child to go on the visit.

Yours sincerely,

Class teacher

✂ -

Visit to ——————

I give my permission for my child to go on the above visit.
Signed ——————

I do not give my permission for my child to go on this visit.
Signed ——————

I should be willing to accompany the class to help on the visit.

Please tick if willing to help. ☐

Seasonal sheet

Seasonal sheet

SUMMER

Seasonal sheet

Seasonal sheet

Autumn

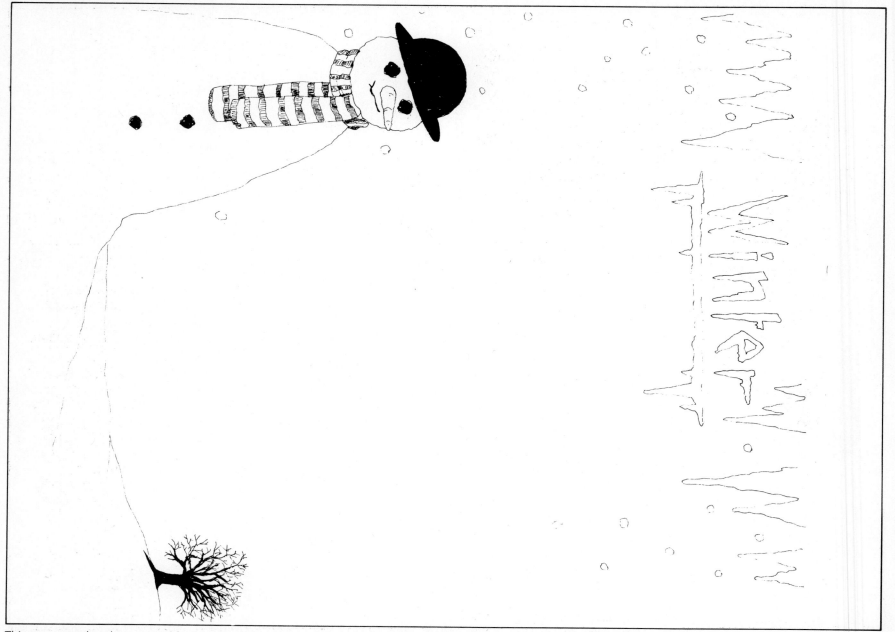

Seasonal sheet

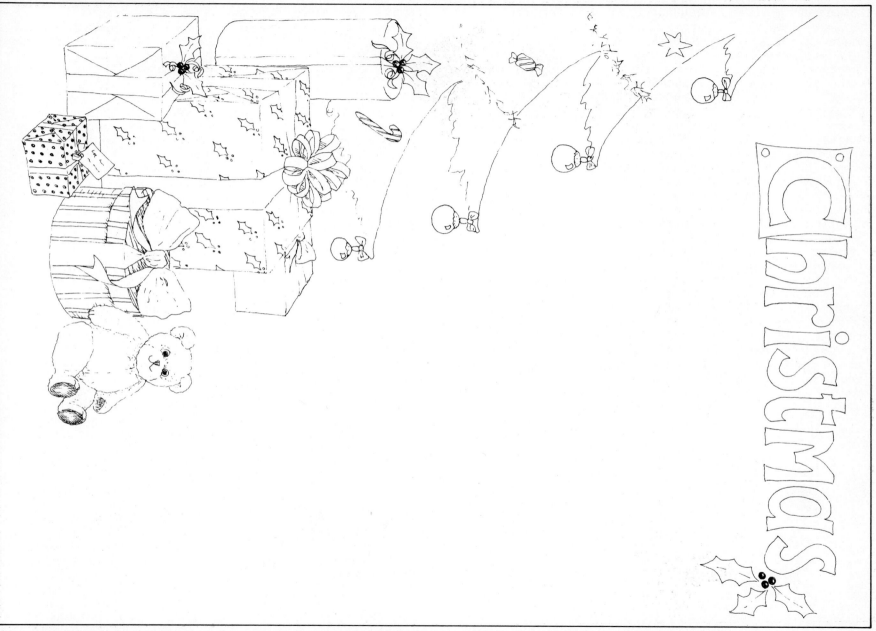

Dates to remember

January
Named after the Roman's two-faced God, Janus, who could look back into the old year and on into the future.
1 New Year's Day.
1 Ganjitsu, the New Year Festival in Japan.
6 Epiphany (Christian), when the infant Jesus is said to have been shown to the Wise Men.
6 Also Twelfth Night.
6 Christmas Eve for Eastern Orthodox Christians.
7 Eastern Orthodox Christmas Day.
19 Eastern Orthodox Epiphany.
25 Burns' Night in Scotland.
● Chinese New Year Festival, ending with Teng Chieh, the lantern festival.

February
The name comes from *Februare*, to cleanse.
2 Candlemas, the Christian festival commemorating the presentation of Jesus in the temple at Jerusalem.
14 St Valentine's Day.
17 George Washington's birthday (Holiday USA).
● Collop Monday and Shrove Tuesday, when Christians feast before Lent.
● Ash Wednesday marks the start of Lent.
● Lent, when Christians observe 40 days of penance and prayer.
● Eastern Orthodox Christians celebrate Butter and Cheese week before Lent.
● Purim commemorates the deliverance of the Jews from Persia by Esther.

March
The month is named after Mars, the Roman God of War.
1 St David's Day, Patron Saint of Wales.
17 St Patrick's Day, Patron Saint of Ireland.
25 Lady Day.
● Mothering Sunday, the fourth Sunday in Lent. Pesach (Passover), when the Jews celebrate their deliverance from slavery in Egypt by Moses.
● Holi, the five-day Hindu Spring festival remembering the love of Krishna and Radha.
● Holy Week, from Psalm Sunday to Easter Sunday, the time for Christians to think of Christ's suffering, death and resurrection.

April
A name derived from the Latin 'to open', *aperire*.
1 All Fools' Day.
4/5 Ch'ing Ming, the Chinese Festival of Pure Brightness, when graves are tended and ancestors honoured.
13 Baisakhi, the Hindu and Sikh festival marking the religious New Year.
23 St George's Day, Patron Saint of England.

May
Possibly named after Maia, the Roman Goddess linked with growth and increase.
1 May Day festivals.
29 Oakapple Day.
● Wesak, when Theravada Buddhists celebrate the birth of their founder, Siddartha Gautama.
● Ascension Day, celebrated by Christians 40 days after Easter.
● Whitsun (Christian).
● Trinity Sunday, the first Sunday after Whit Sunday.
● Corpus Christi, the Thursday after Trinity when Roman Catholics celebrate Christ's presence amongst them.
● Shavuoth or Pentecost, when the Jews celebrate being given the Ten Commandments.

June
Named after Juno, the goddess of beauty and marriage.
21 Summer Solstice and the longest day.
24 Midsummer Day.
● Father's Day (normally middle Sunday of June).
● World Children's Day.

Islamic Festivals
Islamic festivals fall on different days each year as they follow the cycle of the moon.
● Ramadan, when Muslims fast from one new moon to the next and do not eat or drink from sunrise to sunset.
● Eid-ul-Fitr, the Muslim festival when the end of Ramadan is celebrated.
● Eid-ul-Adha which celebrates the Abraham and Isaac story.
● Lailat ul-Bara'h or the Night of Forgiveness, the Muslim feast held on the night of the full moon two weeks before the start of Ramadan, in preparation.

Dates to remember

July
Named in honour of Julius Caesar.

4 Independence Day (USA).

14 Bastille Day (France).

15 St Swithun's Day, when the weather in Britain is supposed to determine the climate for the next 40 days.

25 St Christopher's Day, patron saint of travellers.

● Chinese Festival of Maidens, when young girls pray to the Gods that they will marry loving husbands!

August
Renamed by the Romans after their first emperor, Augustus.

1 Lammas Day, a Christian festival celebrating the harvest.

15 Assumption of the Blessed Virgin Mary (Roman Catholic).

● Janmashtami, a Hindu festival celebrating the birth of Krishna.

● Anniversary of the Guru Granth Sahib, holy scriptures of the Sikhs.

● Raksha Bandham, a festival for Hindu sisters and brothers.

● Yue Lan, the Chinese feast of Hungry Ghosts.

September
Seventh month of the Roman year, which thus gets its name from the Latin for seven *septem*.

28 Feast of St Wenceslas.

29 Michaelmas, the Christian feast of St Michael the Archangel.

● Rosh Hashanah, the Jewish New Year.

● Yom Kippur, the Jewish Day of Atonement.

● Succoth or Sukkot, the Jewish Feast of Tabernacles (harvest festival).

● Chung Ch'iu, the Chinese feast of the moon goddess or Mooncake Festival.

● Durga Puja, when Hindus honour the goddes Durga for nine days and nights.

October
Eighth month of the Roman calendar, the name derived from *octo*, Latin for eight.

31 All Hallows' Eve or Hallowe'en.

● Autumn harvest festival (Christian).

● Diwali, the Indian new year Festival of Light when Hindus remember the reunion of Rama with Sita and their victory over Ravana and the Sikhs celebrate the building of the Golden Temple at Amritsar.

November
The ninth month of the year for the Romans, from the Latin for nine *novem*.

1 All Saints' Day, when Christians remember important figures in Christianity.

5 Guy Fawkes Night (UK).

30 St Andrew's Day, Patron Saint of Scotland.

● Thanksgiving Day in America (held on fourth Thursday of the month).

● Advent Sunday, beginning preparations for Christmas, (celebrated on the Sunday closest to 30 November).

December
Decem is the Latin word for ten.

6 St Nicholas Day when Christians remember the first Santa Claus.

8 Bodhi Day, when Buddhists celebrate Siddartha Gautama becoming the first Buddha.

8 Immaculate Conception of the Blessed Virgin Mary (Roman Catholic).

24 Christmas Eve (Christian).

25 Christmas Day (Christian).

26 Boxing Day and the Feast of St Stephen.

28 Day of the Holy Innocents.

31 New Year's Eve – Hogmanay.

● Birthday of Guru Gobind Singh, a Sikh festival.

● Chanukah or Hannukah, the Jewish Festival of Light.

Welcome card

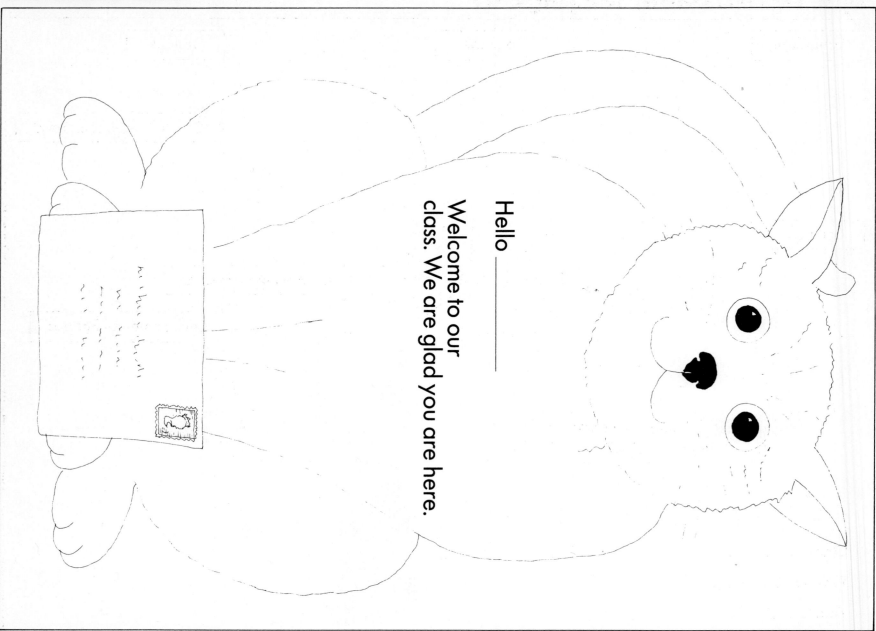

Hello ——

Welcome to our
class. We are glad you are here.

Topic record bank, see page 69

Language

Number

Outings

Difficulties encountered

Science

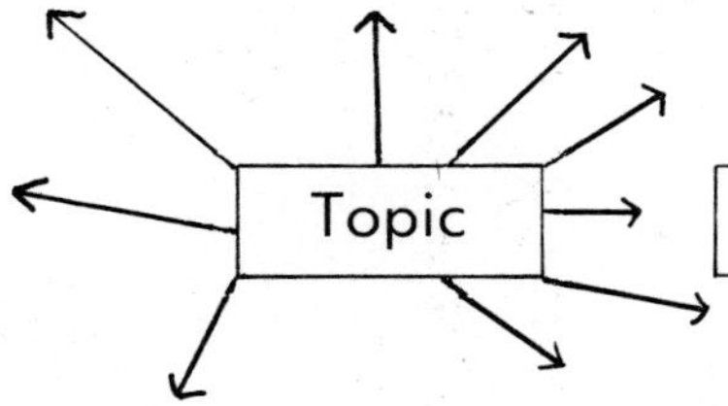

Topic → Music, Movement and PE

Environmental Studies

Religious Education

Art

Class _____

Teacher _____

Year _____

This page may be photocopied for use in the classroom and should not be declared in any return in respect of any photocopying licence.

Other Scholastic books

Bright Ideas
The *Bright Ideas* books provide a wealth of resources for busy primary school teachers. There are now more than 20 titles published, providing clearly explained and illustrated ideas on topics ranging from *Spelling* and *Maths Games* to *World of Work* and *Using Books in the Classroom*. Each book contains material which can be photocopied for use in the classroom.

Teacher Handbooks
The *Teacher Handbooks* give an overview of the latest research in primary education, and show how it can be put into practice in the classroom. Covering all the core areas of the curriculum, the *Teacher Handbooks* are indispensable to the new teacher as a source of information and useful to the experienced teacher as a quick reference guide.

Management Books
The *Management Books* are designed to help teachers to organise their time, classroom and teaching more efficiently. The books deal with topical issues, such as *Parents and Schools* and organising and planning *Project Teaching*, and are written by authors with lots of practical advice and experiences to share.

International Bookshelf
The *International Bookshelf* is a selection of informative educational books available in the UK exclusively through Scholastic. Truly representative of international thinking, these books are classics in their own field.

Let's Investigate
Let's Investigate is an exciting range of photocopiable activity books giving open-ended investigative tasks. Designed to cover the 6 to 12 year old age range, these books present progressively more difficult concepts and many of the activities can be adapted for use throughout the primary school. Detailed teachers' notes outlining the objectives of each photocopiable sheet and suggesting follow-up activities have been included.